DATE DUE			
Nov 6 '72			
Nov 14 '75			
Aug 9 '77			

PARENT GUIDANCE IN THE NURSERY SCHOOL

MARGARETE RUBEN

written in collaboration with

Martha Dancoff • Laura Ellis • Shirley Garber
Iona Kaplan • Florence Loeb • Jane Manning
Ruth Pearce • Barbara Senfeld

Foreword by
ANNA FREUD

INTERNATIONAL UNIVERSITIES PRESS, INC.

New York

CONTENTS

FOREWORD

Margarete Ruben's small handbook on Parent Guidance
does not really stand in need of special recommendation.
It is as serious in purpose as it is modest in appearance
and, as it seems to me, it cannot fail to satisfy a demand
and fill a gap, while conveying simultaneously an accurate picture of the carefulness which the author and her
co-workers exercise when meeting the individual mother's
need.

The professional readers of this publication, whether
workers or authors in the same field, will have no difficulty in recognizing the basic analytic tenets which form
the background of the counseling: the role of the body
needs for food and sleep; the infant's attachment to
the mother; the emotional importance of intake and
elimination; the sequences in the development of sex and
aggression; the conflicts and complexes arising from the
child's ties to his objects, etc. The author shows con-
vincingly that, to her, parent guidance means to draw
on this fund of knowledge, without ever dispensing more
than the mother in question can assimilate at the given
moment.

Many years ago, when some analytic colleagues and I
made our first contacts with the field of education, we
frequently found ourselves unable to prescribe the proper

7

course of action for parents, owing to the scanty and tentative nature of the knowledge which we possessed. Today, when many more relevant data are at our disposal, there are other considerations which make us cautious. The most significant of these is an objection which is itself derived from analytic experience. The successful upbringing of a young child, as we know, does not depend on his mother's objective knowledge but on her subjective emotional attitudes; and difficulties of handling the child arise, above all, wherever the mother's unconscious fantasies and leanings, her defenses, conflicts, symptoms, in short her psychopathology, block the way to understanding and appropriate management.

I have no doubt about the truth of this statement. A woman's capacity for mothering is subject to a multitude of complex disturbances, no less so—or even more—than all other human capacities and relationships. On the other hand, I see mothering not only as an instinctive attitude but also as a skilled task, and an increasingly difficult one under present conditions when the actions of mothers are no longer guided by tradition. Intelligent observation, information about basic facts of human development, and understanding of an individual child's behavior, as they are offered in this book, will strengthen the mothers' own good will, even in those cases where they have to struggle with their own emotions.

Margarete Ruben herself stresses in her Introduction that the limits for all counseling are set by the parents' personalities.

Anna Freud, LL.D.

INTRODUCTION

The decision to write this book grew out of my teaching a seminar for nursery school directors and teachers conducted over a period of two years by the School for Nursery Years in Los Angeles, California.* Similar seminars had been sponsored by the School for several years and had gradually led to the high standard of the School's Training Program and to the spread of analytically oriented educational principles followed by other nursery schools. The courses were predominantly conducted by Hanna Fenichel, Margrit Munk, myself, and more recently have also been taught by other members of the Psychoanalytic Institute of Los Angeles.

Frequent discussions about the importance of parent guidance in a nursery school had taken place and many counseling situations had been studied and examined by us. But these discussions had apparently never led to a full and satisfactory understanding of this subject. When in 1956 I was approached by a group of "old timers" to give once more a seminar about the same topic, I reacted

* The School for Nursery Years is a private, nonprofit institution, founded in 1939. Emphasis is placed upon the psychoanalytic approach to child development.

The Teacher Training Program of the School for Nursery Years, established by its Board of Directors in 1947, is carried out by a qualified faculty under the supervision of the Education Committee.

The Training Program consists of ten class hours and twenty hours of supervised practice teaching per week, for thirty-nine weeks.

9

with disappointment. However, the justification for this request was made clear when I was told that the successful training of their students was hampered by a lack of literature in this area. It was then that I challenged the group to write this booklet.

Although this teaching experiment demanded considerably more time and effort than I had anticipated, it was also a stimulating and rewarding experience. I became aware of the fact that the theoretical presentation of the child's development was easily formulated by the participants. However, when we came to advising the mother, some of the seminar members still revealed misconceptions about the role of instinctual drives in a child. Only after repeated discussions did we arrive at the satisfactory solution presented in this book.

In the last decade, analytically oriented parent meetings and informal discussions among educators, as well as books and pamphlets about dynamic psychology, have dealt with the role of the parent during the growing-up process of his child. Stress has been laid on the importance of the mother's relationship with her child; but even more detailed suggestions and rules have been laid down for application in typical childhood occurrences, such as weaning, toilet training, illness, etc. However, the spread of psychoanalytic knowledge about the child's complicated growing-up process and the parents' participation should not be limited to the mediums of mass education. For this reason, parent counseling in a nursery school setting offers a unique educational framework for the most favorable application of psychoanalytic findings. The individual formulation of her own child's problem provides the mother with new insight and throws new light on the intricacy of educational endeavors.

At no time in a child's life do problems and crises occur as regularly as in its early formative years, for the child's incessant demands call for immediate gratification, necessary frustration, or hopeful diversion. Much will depend upon the mother's emotional response, as well as on her knowledge about the nature of instinct development, infantile sexuality, and early emotional needs, whether she will embark upon the responsibility of her child's upbringing with the right approach.

In the framework of a nursery school personal contact with the mother is easily established, as the situation per se creates an atmosphere of common interest between mother and teacher. Moreover, the union which exists between the mother and her young child contributes to her receptivity for the teacher's guidance.

However, our experience has shown that although the setting and conditions for our work are most favorable, difficulties inherent in this educational sphere also exist. All mothers have their limitations. Gradually, we learned to respect and to meet a mother's individual capacity for accepting advice and putting it into practice in her own way. Some parents were able to use our recommendations immediately; others could only gradually absorb them. Those who were unfamiliar with our educational approach tested our advice clumsily at first, or on unfavorable occasions, while others applied our suggestions without hesitation and with the greatest skill. Some mothers who were most in need of advice were resistant, reacting to suggestions as though they were criticisms. Other mothers did not seem able to grasp the meaning of our recommendations, although they were presented in very simple terms. Much of a mother's reaction depended on her motives for seeking help. Did she come spontaneously and confidently to the school counselor, or was she seeking more advice to add to that she had been getting from family, friends, or neighbors?

With all these considerations in mind, we were interested in finding certain educational principles which would become our point of departure for each case. We concluded that every mother should be acquainted with the developmental stage of the child at the time his problem occurred, and this should be the background for our discussion. For example, when a parent was concerned about her child's thumb sucking, the discussion started with the developmental aspect of this problem, emphasizing the strength and complexity of an oral instinct. After the mother was able to see her child's problem in the light of analytic knowledge, we confined our suggestions to her specific needs, giving her no more information than she had asked for. This "directive" teaching technique became our educational approach. The results of our recommendations were observed and reflected in the mother's attitude to the adviser and to the child's subsequent actions during schooltime. The question of possible further discussion was left to the mother's own choice. Some parents came back for further elaboration of their problem, while others returned only when they were confronted with new stumbling blocks in the upbringing of their child.

While we collected all these experiences, we became more and more aware of the importance of the adviser's personality and her training in this subtle and intricate parent guidance work. In a chapter at the end of this book we set forth some of the criteria for this responsible task. We developed basic preparatory instructions for different counseling situations, some of which can be taught to the young nursery school teacher. However, we came to the conclusion that only a nursery school director or teacher with long-standing experience and postgraduate training has the necessary professional skills to deal with all the problems and intricacies of this work.

Instead of establishing a curriculum for postgraduate training we offer to the interested reader our "models." They are examples of our own attempts to make use of psychoanalytic educational principles, and we hope that in addition to these, they convey to the reader the necessary individual approach on which our guidance work depends. They are not applicable to any other parent guidance situation with a similar problem because they would not fit any other case. In each case dynamic problems were differently exemplified but always in accordance with the child's conflict and the mother's perceptivity. Our "models" are not verbatim recorded conferences, but they are supposed to reiterate the approach and spirit in which the counseling was conducted.

This book will fulfill its purpose if it serves as a stimulus for further explorations into analytically oriented parent guidance work. These explorations may finally lead to a detailed, scientific evaluation of educational problems which mothers encounter in the upbringing of their children.

I am most grateful to the following co-workers whose participation made this book possible. I want to thank Martha Dancoff, Laura Ellis, Shirley Garber, Iona Kaplan, Florence Loeb, Ruth Pearce, Barbara Senfeld, and Jane Manning. The individual nature of these models was further enhanced by the fact that each is a contribution of one of the above members of our discussion group. I also want to thank Margrit Munk for her interest in our work.

My most grateful thanks are due to Ruth Pearce for her additional editorial support, and her painstaking care in preparing this book for publication.

Margarete Ruben

Los Angeles, California
August, 1958

CHAPTER ONE

THUMB SUCKING

Mrs. C. stopped me outside the office. She was obviously harassed and had impulsively decided to ask for help.

"I know you say that Susie is doing fine in school, but frankly this thumb sucking is getting me down. She never watches TV without her thumb in her mouth, and whenever she's angry or tired she goes and gets her blanket and walks around the house with her mouth stretched out of shape, the blanket and her hair all tangled up. The other day I was feeding the baby and she came out looking like an old dish towel, thumb as usual, and started talking to me, and it was just too much! I put the baby down, pulled her thumb out of her mouth, and gave her a slap. That dissolved her and I felt terrible. But it bothers me. After all, she's three. What if she's still doing it at seven or eight or nine?"

As all nursery school teachers know, Mrs. C's question is neither unusual nor difficult to understand. In our culture, children are expected to "grow up" early, to give up infantile pleasure, to stand on their own feet, be clean, self-sufficient, and sociable. Indeed, even if parents follow their own instincts in these matters and do not press their children too early to mature, they are attacked from all sides by well-meaning relatives, friends, storekeepers, bus drivers, and dentists.

Certainly the nursery school teacher, when approached on such a question, carries a particular responsibility to the parent. Many parents do not know that sucking is a pleasure to the newborn, independent of its value as a means to nourishment; that this pleasure is the foundation for emotional health. It prepares us for the acceptance of our bodies as a source of pleasure, and is the first step toward mastering reality. The hungry, cold, or wet infant can wait for comfort if it has this substitute. Sucking is often instrumental in relieving excitement from within and without so that the infant can fall asleep. Furthermore, it is the road to perception and recognition of the world around him, as the infant learns through touch, smell, sight, hearing, and taste what is part of him and what is not. The baby's first contact with his mother is by way of his mouth and the tactile sensations of the skin.

All pleasures are difficult to give up and no child does it quickly or easily. All children retreat to earlier stages of development under stress, and occasional stress is inevitable and desirable for growth. As a child grows, new skills are acquired (motor, cleanliness, speech), and new body pleasures are discovered. The young child delights in the use of new words and their power, in the increasingly delicate manipulation of tools with his hands. He enjoys the physical sensation of moving his bowels, of

16

controlling the sphincters, of withholding and releasing. Later the genitals will be the dominant zone of pleasure in preparation for adulthood. But this is a gradual process. As new demands are made with understanding and approval, the child gives up old needs for new ones.

By the time a child is four or five we would not be surprised to see him still sucking his thumb when going to sleep or infrequently in moments of fatigue or tension. By six or seven most children have left this need behind them. But comforts and pleasures connected with the mouth are never altogether relinquished. How many adults smoke, drink tea or coffee, chew gum? If thumb sucking occupies the child to the exclusion of other activities, or persists until the age of six, seven, or eight, then it is an expression of conflict that is not being resolved by the child. Susie, however, has no such problem, and will probably give up thumb sucking as she has learned to walk and talk and play with other children.

But the "educational conference" does not end here. We must recognize that all mothers have difficulty in accepting some kinds of behavior, normal as it may be, and we must offer concrete suggestions to eliminate some of the tension.

Mrs. C. knows intuitively that pulling Susie's thumb out of her mouth and slapping her is neither successful nor helpful. This kind of "direct" approach might even perpetuate the thumb sucking. We can make suggestions for an "indirect" approach, demonstrating that it is derived from what we have explained to her about child development.

17

First of all, there is the diversion of oral substitutes—gum, lolly pops, bubble pipes, whistles, etc.

Secondly, Susie has a baby brother. Does she have enough time with her mother these days? All children's infantile wants are reawakened when they see a sibling held and nursed by their mother. In fact, many children who have stopped thumb sucking begin again at this time. Perhaps a special time to be held and read to each day would be possible. How much time can Susie's father give? Recognition and attention from him could make a difference.

How much TV is Susie watching? We know that some TV is unavoidable, that it is an aid to both the mother and child at certain times of day. But it might be wise for a while to limit this occupation which is only an inducement to passive reception and daydreaming, and substitute more active play—clay, crayons, puzzles, blocks. This would not only be a diversion for the hands, but would develop new skills and a more active mastery of tensions.

Does Susie take part in household activities? Could she help set table or put toys away or rock the baby? Here, the need for demands and for recognition of Susie as a three-year-old girl would be fulfilled.

Mrs. C. was surprised and relieved to hear that Susie's behavior was not unique. It was clear, however, that it would take time before it would be acceptable to her. This much was accomplished: she was prepared to look again at her children and to observe them in a new way.

In this conference the teacher was aware of Mrs. C's

needs and limitations and adjusted her goals accordingly. It is hard for many parents to believe or accept the fact that these early impulses are so powerful. Indeed, it is often true that the more powerful the instinct, the more difficult it is for the parent to understand it in her child. But it is to this end that the counselor addressed herself. She began with general information concerning early development, showing the origin of Susie's behavior and placing it within normal limits. She then recognized Mrs. C's feelings by offering specific suggestions to divert and educate Susie to a more mature level of behavior. More important, she demonstrated to Mrs. C. that these suggestions were not merely recipes without context, but were commensurate with that knowledge brought to Mrs. C. at the beginning of the conference.

CHAPTER TWO

THE CHILD AND HIS FOOD

Often the teacher of the two-and-a-half-year-old child hears a mother say, "My child's a poor eater. He had such a wonderful appetite when he was a baby, he couldn't get enough to eat; now he seems to eat less—I'm worried." In order to answer these questions a teacher should have a clear picture of the relationship of young children to their food.

The baby, starting with breast or bottle, takes in nourishment and love through his mouth. For the pleasure of nursing and the physical closeness with the mother make for his first love experience. The deep pleasure in sucking, the satisfaction of a full stomach, brings peace and sleep to the infant—until hunger awakens him for the next feeding, which brings a repetition of the cycle. Only gradually does he become aware of the world outside himself. The mouth, for the first year and a half, is the primary source of pleasure. As the baby grows he finds many other sources of gratification—in making sounds, later to become words; in exploring his environment by feeling, touching, smelling, seeing; and in ex-

tending his affections to other members of his family. But
the foundation for his satisfactions in all other areas of his
life is laid in these earliest experiences, when food
brought him pleasure, love, and life itself.

A healthy baby has a lusty appetite. Appetite for food
is not a steady unchanging urge—nor does it increase in
an orderly gradual fashion, then level off when adulthood
is reached. It is influenced by many things. Biological
factors are important, such as: the changing rate of
growth, illness, amount of physical activity, hunger
(which varies at different meals), and the body's specific
chemical needs.

Superimposed upon biological factors regulating appetite is the mother's attitude. Is she loving, gentle, patient with baby ways? Does she support the progress of
the baby from breast or bottle to cup, to meals at table,
understanding his naturally conservative nature? For the
young child clings to the enjoyed, comfortable gratifications—accepting the new only gradually.

Appetite is also affected by emotions and ideas related
to other experiences in the child's life. For example, at
the time of toilet training he may develop a temporary
aversion to certain foods which remind him of his excre-
ments. As he has just learned to find his feces disgusting,
thoughts about his stool may attach themselves to particular foods. These aversions are usually transitory and
lose significance as the child grows older.

The following conference with Johnny B.'s mother is
an excellent example of the parent's need for understanding in this area. Mrs. B. approached me about "Johnny's

21

eating problem" soon after he came to school. Johnny seemed a happy active boy, and his mother generally accepting of him.

On sitting down to talk, I asked her first to tell me all he ate. It seems he had three meals a day, including: meat, cereals, eggs, fruit, and milk, with an occasional snack in between meals. When his mother catalogued the foods she was already somewhat relieved for there was more variety than she originally thought.

I explained that although Johnny is eating less food now than he did at a year and a half, he is not growing as fast now as he did then. His food needs at this time are perhaps not as great. We discussed his absolute refusal to eat cooked vegetables. Learning that fruits are an adequate substitute, and realizing that Johnny enjoyed celery sticks, raw carrots, and lettuce occasionally, helped Johnny's mother to understand that he was getting his minerals and vitamins anyway.

In our discussion we touched on the size of portions— which should be kept small. That young children like to help themselves, whenever possible. That often toast pushers help. That sometimes they refuse to eat at all when unwanted food is on their plate. That they cannot sit for too long. All these are helps to enjoyable eating experiences.

This conference succeeded in showing Johnny's mother that he had no eating problem after all! However, if her anxieties had not been allayed, her own emotional attitude may have finally created a real disturbance in Johnny's pleasure in food.

The reader should be aware that only rarely is a conference as uncomplicated as the one above. Often a seemingly "simple" problem can involve many areas of a child's life. Just one example out of many: a child who refuses food may be revenging himself upon a parent for fancied or real injuries.

Through years of experience, and the intuitive knowledge gained in her work, the counselor learns to assess accurately the situation at hand.

CHAPTER THREE

TOILET TRAINING

Mrs. L. arrived early for her introductory conference. Her son, Peter, three and a half years of age, was to enter school in two weeks. A neat, handsome, friendly woman, she seemed almost at ease. She responded enthusiastically to questions about her son, and had no trouble recalling his history from birth.

Mrs. L. had enjoyed Peter's infancy, and apparently Peter's progress and adjustment in sleeping, eating, motility and communication had been easy.

It was only as we approached the second year of life, the problem of controls and limits, and specifically the subject of toilet training, that Mrs. L. showed concern. "Frankly," she said, "this is the only thing that has come between Peter and us. From the beginning Peter was rebellious and defiant about being trained. I cajoled him, teased him, and in the end even threatened him into using the toilet. My husband was disgusted with me—he thinks I'm not strict enough anyway. It's still anything but a pleasant topic in our family." I asked her when "the beginning" was.

"I started him when he was a year old, but he was actually scared of the toilet, so I stopped. A few months later I tried again, and then it seemed to me he would deliberately and secretly move his bowels anywhere *but* where we wanted. Then I would get angry and plead with him. My husband's parents, and my own mother were shocked that he wasn't trained by eighteen months. And I guess I was ashamed. I read Spock and it still didn't matter. I was sure he'd never learn.

"Then suddenly he became constipated and didn't move his bowels for a whole week. The pediatrician told me not to worry, although my mother-in-law wanted me to give him a laxative. And just as suddenly a week later he sat on the toilet and that was it! Now that I look back on it, I think he was constipated just to get even with us. But you know, he's still finicky, and afraid of other people's bathrooms, and I feel that something was lost between us. He won't let me do anything for him, and when *I* ask him to do something he doesn't listen. He never comes in when I call him, and the other day he went around the block without telling anyone."

Since Mrs. L. was aware of her own anxieties about toilet training, and seemed intuitively to understand her son, two ideas were offered at this time. Mrs. L. needed some reassurance that she could depend on her own feelings reinforced with some information. I said that from what she had told me, her early good relationship with her son seemed well established and that this difficulty would probably be resolved too. Toilet training is not an isolated learning experience but dependent on many factors, not the least of which is a good foundation in the first year of life. I pointed out that it is hard to stand up against relatives, when motherhood is such a new experience and each generation approaches it so differently. Yet Mrs. L. did the right thing in postponing Peter's toilet training when he was afraid. Many children are afraid of toilets. Some are frightened by the noise, some fear the loss of their bowel movement as a part of themselves, some fear that they themselves might fall in the toilet.

It was important, too, to prepare Mrs. L. for some changes in Peter's behavior on entering nursery school. As nursery school teachers know, children often regress at this time. It was easy to predict that Peter might become more irritable and difficult at first and that he might return to just those habits that most distressed those he loved. By warning Mrs. L. of this possibility several aims were accomplished. Should any of these predictions come to pass Mrs. L. would be less surprised and less recriminating. Her faith in the teacher would be strengthened. Her willingness to learn and to co-operate with the school would be increased. To be prepared was the first step to understanding. Another conference was suggested for a few weeks after Peter entered school.

Peter arrived in school, a bright, cheerful, well-organized child. He related easily to adults and was sought after by the children for his good ideas. But his mother was right. It took almost all of Peter's courage to use the bathroom at school. It was only the greater fear of soiling himself that made it possible. For a three-and-a-half-year-old boy, Peter had too difficult a time getting dirty. He would not touch clay, paints, wet sand, or any of the "messy" materials a nursery school offers. As time went on we noticed more. Just as he wanted things clean, he wanted things in order. He was "finicky" as his mother had described him. Even his play ideas had to be carried out exactly as he planned them, which often led to conflict with the other children, and frustration. And although he liked adults and trusted them, he often tested them in routines with a passive resistance reminiscent of Mrs. L's statement: "He doesn't listen." At home he did regress. He was negative, stubborn, and started wetting his pants.

How well this mother had described her own child: Mrs. L. understood much about Peter's conflicts over toilet training, and was intuitively aware of the relationship between this experience and many of Peter's character traits—his stubbornness, defiance, and compulsiveness. But on one important fact in child development she needed enlightenment: the nature and strength of the child's instinctual drives. Without this knowledge Mrs. L. would not be able to form an integrated picture of her child, nor would she be able to cope with these problems in an understanding, practical way.

At our second conference with Mrs. L. we explained that Peter was still fighting the old battle of toilet training. The demands and frustrations connected with the new school situation were undoubtedly the reasons for his recent regression, but this could be turned into an asset rather than a liability.

27

It was at this point that we discussed the rate and sequence of stages in a child's emotional and physical development. It was suggested that all physical processes —like eating, sleeping, and exercise—not only serve the infant's needs for life and growth, but serve his need for pleasure too. It is hard for most adults to understand that moving the bowels is an enjoyable process to the child, particularly as he matures and can control his sphincters, withholding and expelling at his own will. In the second year of life the child has gained considerable mastery over his body. This control of the body, this new motility, is the first step to control of the environment. Now the child can actively seek pleasure and avoid pain, abandoning many of the needs and satisfactions that were part of the passive experience of the infant.

It is in this emotional and physical climate that toilet training is begun. The child wants to comply with the adult he loves and needs, but he also wants to test his new powers. He wants his parents' love and approval, but he also wants this new pleasure regulated only by himself. Over a period of time the child and parents compromise; they demand, give, submit, resist, and finally reach a *modus vivendi*. This period, then, is the testing ground for future social relationships.

Peter's control was perhaps prematurely established. More important, however, was that although established, Peter had not accepted it fully. There were still needs to be satisfied. Mr. and Mrs. L. were willing to let things take their course and not chastise Peter for his present behavior. It was suggested that he be encouraged to play with water and mud and sand in good weather. Many mothers find clay and paints too messy for home use, but certainly colored dough, plasticine, and water colors would be acceptable.

It would be wise to reduce the demands for order and cleanliness for the time being. Of course, limits must be set where danger exists, as when Peter leaves the yard without permission. But as Peter tests his limits and finds them consistent and reasonable, we can expect him to conform to the demands of his parents and his culture.

As the conference came to a close, I reminded Mrs. L. of her plaintive remark at the first interview: "I feel that something was lost between us." I showed Mrs. L. that much of what was lost then was infancy. "As children gain controls, become active rather than remain passive, they become independent. Your child needs you less, obeys you less, but loves you just as much."

This conference would not have been possible without a clear picture of Peter in school combined with a fairly detailed developmental history. With this background it was relatively easy to understand the source and nature of Peter's difficulties and to describe them to Mrs. L. in a simple way.

For Mrs. L. this aspect of her child's development may never be entirely free of tension, but the knowledge gained will serve her well. Her attention was now where it should be, on Peter's individual development, and her goals will be far more easily accomplished as she learns to adjust her educational methods to his needs.

CHAPTER FOUR

AGGRESSION

Mrs. G. came to see me about her four-year-old boy. "I need help," she said, "because Michael has become difficult to manage. He is very aggressive and unpredictable. He can be lovable, sweet, and fun to be with; then at times, especially if I stop him from doing what he wants, he has a temper tantrum. Sometimes he ignores me and just disobeys. When he gets angry he uses bad language and even calls me names. He gets *so* stubborn when I try to make him do what I want. . . ."

"How do you handle him when he becomes rebellious?" I asked.

"Well, I usually try to talk him out of it. Sometimes it works, but I usually wind up screaming or spanking him."

"How long does it take him before you need to scream or spank him?"

"Oh, not right away. I'm usually very patient, but after twenty minutes or so I get tired of diverting him and that's when I get very angry. I don't know what has gotten into him. It was so easy to divert him when he was younger. Now it just doesn't work!

"I can't give in to him all the time, can I? It frightens me when I see how angry he gets. He is so strong. I can hardly stop him. He won't let me do anything for him. I must say he is very capable, but if I leave him alone and let him do what he wants—he gets into trouble. Yesterday he wanted to paint something and insisted on real paint. I talked him out of it, of course. Instead, I gave him a paint brush and a can of water—like you do at nursery school. I was busy cleaning the house and when I called him in for dinner, he came in covered with paint. I ran out to the garage, and sure enough he had gotten into a can of paint and had covered the fence and the incinerator with it. I was so upset and angry I spanked him. I don't think children should be so destructive. Isn't it important to teach them to obey, respect property, and get along with others? We always try to be reasonable and give Michael logical explanations. We never say no without giving good reasons. He never hears bad language at home—where does he get it from?

"I don't like to scream, or spank him—it makes me feel bad. I know we aren't handling him well; that is why I decided to come to you for help. I don't like aggression; but I don't know what to do about it."

Mrs. G. seemed quite distressed, so I commented, "I think coming for advice is a very wise thing to do. Michael's behavior may not be as unusual as you think. It is not easy to understand aggression in children." I started to explain that aggression was a normal part of growth. It starts at infancy as a force within the child that enables him to grow and develop. Without it the child could not learn to cope with his environment. The infant shows aggression when he reaches out, grabs for objects, and puts things into his mouth. He needs to suck and bite. Putting objects into his mouth is his way of exploring his environment. He spits out what isn't pleasing to him and hangs on to what he likes. As he grows older his aggression is put to the service of his curiosity and he gets into everything. He learns that way.

Around the time he is being toilet trained, he makes important discoveries: that by giving and withholding at his own will, he can control the grownups. If they interfere, he responds with temper tantrums, stubborn and defiant behavior.

Gradually, as he grows older, he adopts more socially acceptable means of expressing himself, although he still hasn't given up kicking and pushing at times. As he learns to use language and enjoys it, it becomes a substitute for action, a more mature way of tackling the world. True, it is often bad language, but it expresses his primitive feelings.

Around the age of four, boys particularly need to show how strong they are. They need to express the beginning of manliness. This is important for their future role in society. The many things they have learned to do give them feelings of independence. They need to test their independence and strength in order to continue to develop as Michael had when he painted the fence. Mrs. G. needed to understand that her son has reached this phase. Although he seems to be quite rebellious, there is no real evidence of his destructiveness. Instead, he is expressing a strong need for more physical activity, independence, and admiration.

It seemed to me that Mrs. G. was rather relieved to see Michael's behavior as a normal expression of striving for masculinity. But still she felt helpless in dealing with it; so I became a little more explicit.

"I would recommend that you give Michael every opportunity to express his independence and capabilities. Let him help you with chores that seem to interest him —burning paper in the incinerator with your supervision, planting and watering in the garden, and participating in any activity with his father that he can enjoy. Physical play would be very good for him at this time, such as ball playing, darts, climbing equipment, running, jumping.

"It is also very important for Michael that decisive limitations are set for him by you and your husband. For example, he does not have to use bad language anywhere at any time. I think you will find it much easier to get along with him if you maintain a consistent and firm position in handling him."

In giving Mrs. G. more explicit suggestions for helping Michael, my goal was to reinforce what understanding of aggression Mrs. G. already had. It became apparent that "appeals to reason" are certainly less effective in dealing with Michael's behavior than support and encouragement for his productive activities, plus definite limits to help keep in check his potentially destructive impulses.

CHAPTER FIVE

THE TIMID CHILD

At staff meeting, the teacher of the three-and-a-half-year-olds made a suggestion. "I think we should ask for a conference with Kay's mother. Kay is beginning to make some progress at school, and we should explain to her mother what we are doing. Maybe she can tell us what has been going on at home."

Kay had been in school five weeks, and the change had indeed been marked. She came into our school a pale child, with large eyes, watching the children carefully, but too shy to attempt to do anything herself. All overtures of friendship from the other children had made her hold more tightly onto her mother, and when her mother left, she transferred her hand to the teacher, and timidly followed her around.

The knowing teacher had proceeded with gentleness and reassurance. She knew that some shyness is natural, and usually temporary. A new child needs a chance to assimilate the varied experiences that nursery school offers. For some children, the friendly overtures of the others are all that is needed to change the first experiments into active participation.

But Kay's teacher had seen her withdraw, afraid and unable to accept an interested child. She had seen her stand at the foot of the ladder, looking anxiously and wistfully to the top. And the teacher knew that she herself would have to use caution, time, and understanding. Kay needed confidence in herself before she could go out to others, or play on any of the equipment.

And so, Kay had proceeded at her own pace. She had been offered neither excessive sympathy, urging, nor disapproval. Instead, her teacher had been friendly and encouraging in a relaxed way. When Kay looked undecided at the ladder, her teacher said, "When you're ready to climb, I'll watch," and "I'll hold onto you when you want to try," thus giving that needed extra support and encouragement in trying something new. Social contacts were also not forced, nor neglected. At juice time, Kay's teacher pointed out to her that Jane was offering another cookie. "Jane likes you, she is your friend." These are the sorts of statements that made Kay aware that the world around her was open for opportunities to explore and enjoy. They put the responsibility for such enjoyment on her, assuring her that she could decide for herself, and that she was accepted as she was.

Kay's mother came to school for the interview we had requested. An intense woman, older than most mothers of that group, she clutched her purse tightly, and sat rigidly at the edge of her chair as if expecting criticism of her capabilities as a mother. Kay had been placed in nursery school, Mrs. M. said, because she was whiny and uncooperative at home. She always followed her mother around, never would stay in her own room and play, but carried her toys all over the house. Mrs. M. admitted that she had set ways and prided herself on her lovely house. Mrs. M. said she was old to have had her first, and probably only child. She thought that perhaps her age had made it hard for her to be at ease with her child, but she never imagined that she would have such an unhappy one.

"When did this start?" Mrs. M. was asked. Mrs. M's face softened. "I'd almost forgotten what an adorable baby she was. Quiet, she slept a lot. We had such cute baby clothes for her. We rocked her and played with her all the time she was up. But when she started to crawl she began to get into everything. At first, she picked up everything and put it in her mouth. Then she began to break things. Several good ash trays. But she cried if I kept her too long in her playpen. The worst part was that she was always getting dirty. I had to change her clothes three or four times a day."

"What about toilet training?" she was asked. Mrs. M. hesitated, embarrassed. "My pediatrician told me it was all right to start training her at eighteen months. I watched her carefully, and put her on the potty regularly. Once I started, I almost always caught her in time, and I remind her now, although she's pretty good about remembering to go herself.

"You know," Mrs. M. added, "my husband and I can't get over how much more pleasant she's been since she's been going to school. The first week she kept saying she didn't want to go without me, now she doesn't even say good-by. How can I make her this happy at home?"

Mrs. M. was congratulated on the attention and loving care Kay had received during her infancy. She was also reassured in hearing that many mothers experienced the same distress and feeling of ineffectiveness when their first children entered the "age of motility." Had she known what to expect, and had she been more informed as to how to meet this new behavior, she would surely have coped with it with more equanimity.

Children like and need to explore—to explore themselves and to explore their environment. The way they explore, by adult standards, is sometimes considered "dirty" or "naughty." But this is part of growing up. The things that Kay had done were normal and universal. Putting everything in her mouth is typical of a crawling infant. Getting dirty, enjoying messiness, even smearing at times is natural at the time the child is learning self-control and cleanliness. If a child feels he is disapproved of, if he feels his natural impulses are bad, this fear could extend to all areas of behavior, and so he might whine and seek constant adult approval.

"Do you mean that I should let her play with mud all over the house?" Mrs. M. asked defensively.

"Certainly not!" was the reply. An overindulgent parent can also make a child fearful. Some parents have misunderstood acceptance of a child to mean no controls whatsoever, and to mean complete indulgence of a child's demands. Frustrations are the cornerstone of learning; all children are eager to learn, eager to grow up. What

Mrs. M. had to do was become aware of Kay's instinctual drives, respect their strength, and allow for their expression or substitution at reasonable times. Kay could wear washable jeans to play in, and pretty frocks worn on special occasions could then be expected to be kept clean. Out of doors, and at nursery school, she could play with clay and mud; at home, washing dishes in soapy water might be more suitable, and something Mrs. M. could more easily supervise and accept.

Now Mrs. M. for the first time sat back in her chair. She was quiet for a few moments, and then said slowly, "Have you any more suggestions?"

Once Mrs. M. found herself able to respond to the teacher's advice she wanted even more of it. Her confidence in the school had developed through observing her child's progress, and it is unlikely that any faster way could have produced as satisfactory results. Kay's mother needed to watch her child's growing happiness and share with her the school experience in order to relax her overly high standards. Too precipitous an approach might have frightened this tense mother away completely.

This is an important aspect of all work with parents. Many times inexperienced counselors want to move too rapidly; they see something wrong and the urge to put it right is irresistible. It is good to remember that success in this field is, as a rule, not measured in immediate results, but in changes effected over a longer period of time.

CHAPTER SIX

THE NEW BABY

Children communicate in many ways—by gesture, by words, and by their play. The little girl of three or four, who puts on boys' clothes and pretends she is a cowboy or a policeman, does not have to tell her mother or her teacher that she wants to be a boy. Sometimes a child's behavior is not so evident by itself, but when the mother's report is considered too, they tell the alert teacher a clear story. Such is the case in this conference about Janet B.

Janet had been in school since the age of three. She was an only child of young, intelligent parents. From the beginning Janet was vivacious, curious, and creative. It had always been somewhat difficult for her to share and take turns with other children, and she had always displayed a tendency to test her limits with the teacher. This, however, was balanced by her positive response to the approval of her peers and teachers, her sense of logic and reality, and her genuine enthusiasm about all activities. In short, her personality was very much a reflection of her position in the home with doting parents.

At the time of this conference Janet was four and her whole world was about to change. Her mother was seven months pregnant and excitedly looking forward to a second child.

In school at this time Janet had great swings in mood —from extreme anger to great excitement to periods of lassitude and sadness. In doll play with her friend Jean she had been unwilling to give up her role as mother to give Jean a turn, a compromise she had learned to make some time earlier.

Instead, when she took issue with her friend she would burst into tears and leave screaming. A short time later she would excitedly and with much giggling stuff clothes and rags under her shirt and jeans and strut about the room. At lunch one day she said she couldn't eat peas because she'd "get a baby."

Mrs. B. asked for a conference because she had found herself impatient and dissatisfied with Janet, who demanded constant attention just at the time when Mrs. B. seemed to need more time for herself and was feeling particularly tired. She said that she had told Janet about the approaching baby, but Janet had shown no interest. "In fact, she seems not to listen. But whenever I sit down to read or just rest she bombards me with questions and demands."

"Questions about the baby?" the teacher asked.

"Oh no, questions about everything else—and she isn't interested in the answers—only in getting my attention."

The teacher could see that Mrs. B. sensed that Janet's behavior was connected with the approaching baby, and that the mother was more nonplused by the lack of direct concern that Janet showed than by the annoying behavior. After all, if Janet could only express her fears, or would only ask questions, it would be easy for Mrs. B.

to know what to do. In this conference it would be the
teacher's task to explain Janet's confusion of thoughts
and feelings relating to the new baby, to show that these
confusions are for the most part inevitable, and to let
Mrs. B. see that, in fact, Janet was communicating as
directly as she knew how.

When children are told of a baby growing inside the
body of their mother, they can be only dimly aware of
what this means. They observe their mother's growing
tummy and automatically conclude that the baby entered
through the mouth, and will come out through the anus
in accordance with their own bodily experiences. They
hear talk about going to the hospital and wonder about
frightening events there. For instance, they might equate
childbirth with the body bursting or exploding. The
child's intellectual concepts are entirely logical within
his limited understanding of external events. Reassurance
that one does not get a baby by eating peas, that nothing
will happen to the mother, will alleviate some of the
anxiety. It is important to explain to Janet that the baby
is in a special place (not mixed up with the food) and
will come out a special way. But this information will by
no means eradicate all the misconceptions, because children cannot think in different terms yet. The child of
four is not ready for information about conception.

But no child thinks in a vacuum. Janet's thoughts
about the baby were complicated by a myriad of feelings
connected with it. To be sure, she, in part, looked forward
with pleasure to a baby to play with. She was aware of her
mother's joy and anticipation, and wished that she too

could have a baby. Indeed, she often played that she was the mother, that she was pregnant. But this was not a game free of anxiety, so clearly shown by the giggling and excitement at school. Mixed up with her wishes to be mother, herself, were her fantasies about childbirth, and her fears for her mother. And of course deep within her was the fear of being displaced by a rival and hence losing her mother's love. If she could have expressed it, she would have said, "I don't want mother to have a baby. I want to be the only one." Fear, anger, envy, confusion, and a little delight were Janet's emotions at this time.

The arrival of the baby will alleviate many of her apprehensions, making a reality of a presentiment. As a matter of fact, it is possible that Janet will accept with joy the new baby at first. Often children are not jealous until many months later when the baby is old enough to demand more time and take part in the daily routine or even later when the baby interferes with Janet's activities. But then her jealousy will be of flesh and blood. What is hard for her now, and for her mother too, is that Janet has no clear idea of what it is that bothers her. She asks her mother questions to get her attention, to make her angry, and because there are the big questions that she doesn't know how to ask. It will be much easier for Mrs. B. to deal with this behavior now that she can understand what is going on in her child and that these dim expectations are inevitable.

But above all, Janet must learn to accept reality. Frustration and disappointment are as much a part of life as pleasure and success.

CHAPTER SEVEN

MASTURBATION AND FANTASY

Mrs. Rogers, the mother of a four-year-old boy, came to my office one Tuesday. "May I have a conference with you as soon as possible? I would like to talk with you about Paul, because suddenly he has started to masturbate." We arranged an appointment for 10 A.M. on the following Thursday. I did not want to keep Mrs. Rogers waiting too long. She seemed quite concerned. During the interim, I had the opportunity to review my knowledge of a subject which is often difficult to treat in a simple understandable way with parents.

Masturbation is only one manifestation of a long and complicated process of development. Observation and study of young children has shown that there is a gradual, logical, and natural progress in their sexual development as well as in the other phases of their growth. Around three years of age, children become aware of the difference between boys and girls. They will, if permitted, ask questions about it. Little girls wish for a penis. Some of them insist they are growing one. Others try to urinate standing up or indicate in other ways their envy of a boy's masculinity. On the other hand, when little boys see another human being without a penis, they become concerned that something could happen to their own. Children, growing up, cannot assimilate their total environment all at once. They take in bits and pieces of the world in digestible amounts. Often the mind distorts the facts into forms acceptable to the child in terms of his own past experiences, feelings, or wishes. These distortions are perfectly logical to the childish mind.

In attempting to find satisfactory answers to their questions and thoughts about birth, children's fantasies run the gamut. One child, seeing his mother's abdomen grow bigger and bigger, followed by the arrival of a sibling, imagines that she ate something and in that way "got a baby." Another child thinks the mother's stomach is cut open to let the baby out. A third believes the baby appears through the navel. Most interesting is the fact that these fantasies persist even when the truth is given. Often parents are puzzled by this. We know, however, that fantasies serve important functions in the child's life. They reflect his wishes, fears, and anxieties. Telling children the truth at least helps them cope with their fantasies by reinforcing reality for them.

By the time a child reaches four, he knows the difference between boys and girls. He knows where babies come from and, sometimes, how they are born. A few, even at this early age, have asked or thought about the most complicated question of all—that of conception. Between four and five years of age, the child has an idea of the role of the parents. The little boy wants to be like his father. He loves his mother and would like to marry her. Only gradually and unwillingly does he accept the fact that she is already married and he will have to find a wife of his own when he is grown up. A little girl emulates her mother. She would like to marry her father. She would like to have babies.

Four- to five-year-olds have become aware of their genitals through the pleasurable feelings they get when they touch them. They offer consolation during this turbulent phase of growth. Most children seem to find the period before falling asleep a natural time for fantasy and masturbation. Their thoughts are stimulating; physical sensations are aroused. And in fear, anxiety, or excitement, they turn to their bodies for comfort. Not all children limit their masturbation and fantasy to bedtime. Often during the day when tired, when overstimulated, or when the stress of their environment becomes too great, children may resort to their fantasy world and to masturbation. Masturbation and fantasy are ways of expressing pent-up feelings and desires. Physical activities and dramatic play are other ways through which a child can relieve tension.

Usually, when children reach elementary school age, masturbation no longer plays as important a role in their lives. Their early struggles with sexual feelings tend to fade into the background as their energies are focused on learning. They are eager to acquire many new skills— in athletics, manual arts, and scholarship. They want to know more about the world around them and are ready to begin using the tools of their culture.

After reviewing this material I was again overwhelmed by the wealth of experiences the small child must digest in such a relatively short time. I was quite hesitant in deciding how to present to Mrs. Rogers this expression of her child's phase of development. However, Mrs. Rogers, herself, showed me the way by opening the discussion with the remark, "I have read and heard that masturbation is something all children have to go through and that there is nothing wrong when it happens. But it makes me nervous."

Mrs. Rogers expressed her conflict quite clearly. I said, "I think I understand. Although you have read and heard that masturbation is normal, when you see your son masturbate, your feelings become stronger than your reasoning. After all, when we were youngsters, masturbation was regarded as unhealthy, immoral, and dirty. Years ago, parents tried to stop this behavior by threatening, punishing, or condemning their children. It is not easy for us to forget the mores and standards of our own formative years. However, since we know more about children's development these days, perhaps, in time, we can learn to feel differently about this kind of behavior.

"I'm sure you recall our discussion some time ago about the pleasure Paul got when he sucked his thumb—how this part of his body was such a comfort when he was tired, cross, or unhappy. So you remember a parent meeting at which we discussed the pleasure children experience when defecating—how they enjoy learning to control their sphincters, withholding and expelling at their own will? And now, as a four-year-old, Paul has discovered that another part of his body gives him pleasure, namely, his genitals.

"You know, Mrs. Rogers, two other mothers have mentioned seeing their children masturbate. It would probably be wise to discuss this phase of development in more detail with all the mothers of the group. Would you attend such a meeting and contribute your observations and feelings? It may help some of the others to feel freer in talking about masturbation."

It has been our experience in working with parents that topics like masturbation, which arouse intense and uncomfortable feelings, need to be tactfully treated. These subjects are frequently more easily managed in small meetings than in individual conferences. In group situations, anxieties are minimized because feelings and reactions can be shared.

The meeting with the mothers of the four- to five-year-olds took place soon after our conference. Mrs. Rogers attended. When she heard other mothers' reactions to their children's behavior she was surprised and relieved. Many of them felt much the way she did. She was then able to express herself with greater ease and confidence than she had in our earlier meeting.

As leader of the group, I introduced more material on this developmental phase of growth than would have been possible in an individual conference. Many questions arose concerning sexual curiosity and overstimulation. We suggested that it would be wise to protect the child from situations that tend to be overstimulating.

It is best to encourage dressing and bathroom privacy

for all members of the family—if this practice has not already been established. Rough-house play with father should be replaced with less exciting activities. Certainly, getting into bed with the parents should be avoided, as should showering or bathing with adults and older siblings. Most children of this age are capable of washing themselves and taking care of their own bathroom needs.

From some of the remarks made by the mothers after the meeting, I knew they had profited by the open discussion. As one mother commented, "Well, I don't suppose I'll ever be comfortable seeing Robert masturbate —but at least I won't make an issue of it any more."

CHAPTER EIGHT

SLEEP DISTURBANCES

Anna B. had entered nursery school at three years of age. A quiet, but active and contented child, she had made a solid adjustment to the school situation. Except for regular report conferences it was not until Anna was four and a half years old that Mrs. B. came to the school with a special problem. Anna had been waking at night for several weeks, insisting that her father come to her room. Mr. B. would pick her up, and walk the floor with her for as long as an hour before Anna would return to bed.

The teacher reminded Mrs. B. that in the initial interview with her before Anna had entered school, she had mentioned an earlier sleeping disturbance. Mrs. B. remembered it well. "It was when Anna was two. She would waken and call me, apparently afraid of the dark and not wanting to be alone. I somehow thought it might have been connected with being scared by a big dog in the neighborhood. But anyhow as soon as I would come to her she would relax and go to sleep. I found that if I turned on the light in the hall and left the door a bit open she was all right. It disappeared in a week or so. But this time—she won't let me help her at all—only her father. And he would do anything for her. She wakes up afraid, I know, but I think she holds on to him long after she's quieted. She's our only daughter and our baby, you know. I have an idea that there is something we could do to help Anna and all of us get some sleep!"

The teacher reported to Mrs. B. a dream that Anna herself had reported at school. She and her brothers lived all alone in the woods without their mother, cared for by "my wonderful daddy," as she put it. That Anna wanted her "wonderful daddy" all to herself was very clear.

But before discussing this new problem, the teacher thought it wise to begin by explaining to Mrs. B. what had taken place at the time of Anna's first sleeping disturbance. Many children of two experience this feeling of loss and loneliness at night. They are beginning to be aware of a world outside of home and mother. They wish for freedom, even demand it occasionally, but too much can be frightening. Mother must always be there for aid and comfort. It is this fear of separation that wakens the small child at night. The big dog that scared Anna might have intensified her anxieties and have come to represent the dangerous world outside. But her fears, her feelings of loneliness were quickly erased by knowing her mother was there—and later just by knowing her mother was near.

This time Anna's sleeplessness was of an entirely different nature. Just as boys at this time of their development want the exclusive companionship of their mothers, so do girls want their fathers. Many four- to five-year-olds wander into the parental bedroom, wanting many things —food, drink, or just to get in bed with daddy or mother. Anna had gone one step further and gotten her father out of bed completely!

The teacher went on to say that this is not an easy period in a child's life. For along with these strong wishes for the parent of the opposite sex goes a good deal of anger toward the other parent, and the wish that he or she would be out of the way. All children find these wishes shameful and frightening, and many are apprehensive that they may be punished for them. At night, however, they no longer have the conscious controls that are at their disposal in the day, and as a consequence nightmares and sleeplessness take over. Mrs. B. was right in believing that Anna was really afraid when she wakened and called her father. She is in need of comfort against her anxiety; but in not letting her father go, she fulfills her wish to have him to herself.

It was suggested to Mrs. B. that she talk this over with her husband. Perhaps when Anna cries at night Mrs. B. could begin to go to her instead of her father. Anna can learn that her father needs his rest too, and that his place at night is with mother. She will be angry, it will never be easy, but she will accept this frustration in time. It is also likely that she will be relieved, knowing that her parents are setting limits on her wishes. And in many ways Mrs. B. could comfort Anna even better than her husband; for what could be better at such a time than for Anna to know that in spite of her hostile feelings, her mother still loves her? If the parents could share this nighttime burden and be firm with Anna in this regard, the teacher was certain that this sleeping disturbance, like the other, would soon disappear.

In this conference it was thought wise to deal exclusively with Anna's sleeping disturbance. Some teachers might have extended their advice to daytime suggestions to Mrs. B. that would help her daughter through this period.

Advice of this kind could have interfered with Mrs. B's confidence in her role as a mother, a role which she had always filled quite adequately. Mrs. B wanted specific help and this purpose was accomplished. She herself could be relied upon to make use of what general principles she had acquired in this conference.

CHAPTER NINE

JEALOUSY

Last night Mrs. D. phoned me. She sounded upset and unhappy. She said she had to talk to me about Donny, and couldn't wait until tomorrow—her day to transport him to school. She was at her wit's end; Donny's behavior at home was unbearable. Why, just this evening he had broken several of Pam's treasured toys. Recently he seemed always so angry and difficult. How could two children be so different? Pam, even though she wasn't yet two, was such a delight, so agreeable and easy to be with. After all, why couldn't Donny, who was a bright four-year-old, understand that Pam was still a baby and needed a lot of attention from her Mommy? It seemed that every time Mrs. D. busied herself with Pam, he became involved in any number of situations which demanded Mrs. D's attention and took her away from the baby.

As I listened I learned more about Donny's recent behavior. He refuses to go to the bathroom alone, frequently wets himself, and has soiled himself three times this past month. At bedtime he insists upon his mother staying in the room with him long after he has been tucked in. If she attempts to leave, he whines and insists the blankets aren't right or his pajamas have to be changed. Some nights Mrs. D. isn't able to leave his room (which he shares with Pam) until he is asleep. And if she is firm and refuses to comply with his constant demands at bedtime, he cries and wakes his sister. So of course she is forced to sit by his bed until he falls asleep.

During the day when Mrs. D. isn't able to gratify Donny's demands for attention his reaction is persistent whining, complaining, angry tears, and not infrequently a tantrum. If his mother refuses to be moved by these scenes, he resorts to what she called "downright nasty behavior," such as pinching Pam when she refuses to give up her toys, writing on the walls with crayon, and flooding the bathroom when he floats his boats in the tub. Mrs. D. just can't understand what has gone wrong. Before Pam was born she tried to prepare him for the new baby; and did everything the books suggested!

This morning at school there was little opportunity for conversation with Mrs. D. However, it was plain to see that she was upset by her son's aggressive behavior, his low frustration level, his persistent bullying of many of the children. I was sure that she failed to notice his ability at woodwork and his imaginative contributions at story time. I stayed fairly close to Donny most of the morning, not only to help him work through difficult situations involving himself and his peers but also to observe him, so that I could organize my thoughts for this afternoon's conference.

As the conference with Mrs. D. was under way it became apparent that she thought of Donny only as an extremely aggressive child. She could not accept Donny's jealousy because of its appearance at a time when she no longer expected it. Often jealousy of a sibling isn't shown until the younger child is well along in his second year. At this time the baby sleeps less, moves about, participates in family life more, and becomes a more recognizable threat to the older child.

Although most mothers today are informed about sibling rivalry, it is nevertheless difficult for them to recognize it at any given time, for each child expresses it in different ways. Some start to soil again, to wet the bed, to insist upon being fed and in general babied in identification with the newborn. The same feelings can also be recognized in a general whining, demanding, pestering behavior toward the mother. Others dare to show their anger at the intruder by hitting, poking, pinching, or by love pats which are too hard. A secure child may be able to verbalize his jealousy by suggesting that the baby be returned, exchanged, or discarded. However, there are jealous children who, for fear of reprisal, have no direct outlet, but turn it into excessively obedient behavior.

In Donny's case intensification of his jealousy had taken place because he now had reached the stage of his development in which he wanted to be his mother's only loved one.

There are a number of ways Mrs. D. can help her son keep his jealousy within reasonable bounds. Perhaps she can spend some time alone with Donny reading to him, taking him for a walk or a drive, allowing him to choose some special activity they can do together. Scheduling Donny's bedtime a half hour or even an hour later than

Pam's would make bedtime easier for him and his mother. This arrangement could also give Donny more time with his father, or the quiet companionship of both parents all to himself. If the family can arrange to give him a room of his own, play situations at home might be simpler, and bedtime might be a happier time.

Donny's aggressive behavior in school was also a sign of developing masculinity. I pointed out the positive, mature side of his personality, his increasing skills and keen mind. If Mrs. D. knew what to expect of a four-year-old boy, she could begin to show Donny the advantages in growing up. For instance he can talk and Pam is just learning. He is very strong now, he even goes to school.

Mrs. D. is a dependent, rather unaware woman. She reads many books on child care, but is unable to comprehend or apply what they say. I was convinced that the spoken word would be more comprehensible. As I cautiously but clearly gave her a picture of what I felt to be Donny's situation at home and at school, I hoped she would begin to see that the reason for his difficult behavior was his own unhappiness. Why unhappy? Because he felt rejected and displaced, and this was impossible for him to bear.

During the conference Mrs. D. made an honest attempt to look back over the home situation during the past year. She realized that she had not spent much time with Donny and therefore he had reason for his jealousy. What she called aggressive behavior was actually a bid for more attention. She seemed, at the end of the conference, to see her son in a more sympathetic light.

CHAPTER TEN

THE CHILD'S GROWING EGO

Harry's mother came to school for her last conference prior to Harry's "graduation" to kindergarten. This is a regularly planned conference in which most parents expect an evaluation of their child's whole experience in nursery school and suggestions for his future education. The teacher knew Mrs. G. well—a resourceful, loving mother who found it painful and difficult to apply the necessary frustrations and make the realistic demands on her son that are essential for growing up. It was expected, therefore, that this change for Harry from the protected atmosphere of a nursery school to public school would bring up more anxieties in Mrs. G. than in many other mothers.

Mrs. G. was indeed apprehensive. How would Harry do in school? Would he be able to pay attention in class? Will he sit still? Will he obey the teacher? Were these wonderful years in nursery school really preparation for the more rigid school atmosphere he is going to have to adjust to? From this rush of questions she followed with her worried observations of Harry at home. "Lately he has been so restless, busying himself with all sorts of activities that come to nothing. Somehow he reaches out for something which apparently I cannot give him. With his father too—he is always bothering him to do things for him, to fix this or that. Is he like this here in school, too?"

"We have observed something like this in school. Harry is quite imaginative and often begins creative projects, only to flounder before he finishes. We find that we must be there to help him follow through. He needs the encouragement and strength of the teacher to finish a piece of work, and the ultimate pleasure he gets out of his achievements makes us sure that this is the way to help him. I think that what he reaches out for that you feel you cannot give him is support for his ego strength. By making demands and setting limits, encouraging his activities to completion and helping him to overcome obstacles, you accomplish just that. I would like to remind you that, although you have had so much to give Harry, you have also had difficulty withholding, disciplining and demanding. When Harry first came to school you told us that it had taken you so much longer than you would have wished to begin weaning Harry from the bottle, and that you yourself were surprised at how easily it was accomplished when you had the courage to do it. It was the same with the toilet training, yet after much hesitation from you he responded quickly and even with pride.

"A child not only gets pleasure and enjoyment from controlling and mastering his impulses, but he is also hungry for new experiences and new skills of muscle and mind. These very skills in turn help him to grow and develop. For instance, at the time of weaning, the very young child is just beginning to recognize and investigate other objects than the bottle and his mother. By giving him toys, showing him pictures, the mother helps him to expand his horizon, and to separate himself more clearly from these primary needs. With these incentives, when the mother communicates her expectations to the child, he will not hold on to the bottle unnecessarily long.

"At the time of toilet training too, the encouragement to independence, to new muscle activity, and new social experiences is again a stimulus to moving forward. I'm sure you remember when he first came to school, his pleasure in bike riding and climbing. And how amazed you were at the thrill he had shown in doing a puzzle over and over again. You were also pleased to see how well he cooperated with the other children, taking turns and sharing his possessions. To be sure, it is hard to relinquish old satisfactions, but children also *want* to grow up, to be independent and proud of themselves. Only the other day Harry succeeded in building a fire department of blocks which took him almost an hour to complete. He had set himself a rather difficult project—a two-story building with a fire pole inside. Feeling frustrated he decided to build it more simply and leave it at that. We, however, told him that we thought he could build it as planned and that we would help him. In this way he is learning to set goals for himself that he can realistically fulfill. When we indiscriminately approve of all of his accomplishments, we fail to strengthen a child's ego. He knows that some of his achievements are better or more beautiful than others, and he enjoys standards set for him. When Harry bothers his father to do things for him he really means to do things *with* him and to learn *from* him. No child should be pushed into activities that are bound to end in failure, but he must learn that in climbing the ladder of achievement, immediate success is not always forthcoming or necessary.

"In this next step for Harry you will be faced again with at least as difficult a task as in the past. Undoubtedly Harry will struggle against accepting new frustrations and demands. If you remain helpful and consistent in your attitude, without too many verbal explanations, he will accept and find pride in making the necessary step to being a school boy."

To the teacher's great satisfaction Mrs. G. replied enthusiastically, "Finally I understand what you've been trying to tell me for the last two years. I think I've always been afraid to let Harry suffer disappointments or to make him give up pleasures. Actually I've given him too much responsibility for making these steps forward himself. After all, we have the same wish as Harry—to let him grow up. I'm very grateful to you for having pointed this out repeatedly to me. It has taken a long time, but I'm sure I'm on the right track now."

CHAPTER ELEVEN

THE LIMITATIONS OF COUNSELING

Betty E., three years old, was entered in school during the summer session. She was enrolled by her father who was not living at home, as the parents were considering divorce. He came into the office to talk with the director, saying that he felt in a desperate position. He spoke most disparagingly of Betty's mother, and expressed great concern about Betty.

"In my childhood," said Mr. E., "they used to say that a child like this would not live out the winter. She's so quiet, she depresses any group of kids she goes into. Everything becomes silent when she's around."

In school Betty proved to be quite different from her father's description. Far from being silent, she talked incessantly, and attempted to form relationships indiscriminately with every adult in the school. Her nagging, "Where are you going? Are you going to stay here?" and her constant interrupting and mimicking of conversation were distracting to both children and adults. Betty was hard to love. As a matter of fact, she was not at all receptive to affection. When the teacher picked her up she found her rigid, unresponsive, struggling to get down.

As the regular autumn session got under way, Betty's problems seemed to become intensified. The planned activities and tighter routines were difficult for her, and increased her anxiety. Her persistent nagging demands seemed to satisfy several contradictory needs. They were a device to make contact with people, yet one which made any genuine relationship impossible. In addition, it was her only way to express hostility, for Betty never struck out, never cried. Finally, it became a means of filling hours spent at school.

As a first-aid measure, her teacher enlisted the cooperation of staff members. They were not to answer her incessant questions, but were to refer her back to her own teacher. "Ask *your* teacher, Betty, she is here to help you," was to be the general tone. She hoped that Betty might be able to identify with one adult, and one group.

Although Mr. E. was instrumental in bringing Betty to the school, all further communication was with the mother. Mrs. E. was a woman of many affectations. Her dress, language, and general demeanor were highly stylized and theatrical. Although she asked for a conference, arrived promptly and seemed eager, it was soon clear that she needed to control and direct the discussion. She let the teacher know immediately through her use of popular psychological terminology that she was "in the know." But her interpretation of Betty's behavior betrayed her real lack of understanding. She said that Betty had a "photographic memory"—that if an ash tray were placed in a different position on a table, Betty noticed it and insisted it be returned to its original place. She also felt that Betty was "quite a little actress," that she spent much of her time pretending to be someone else, either the children in the group or the teacher. The mother was unable and unwilling to recognize that Betty, in this way, was expressing her own deep need for security and identity.

Mrs. E. tried several times to involve the teacher in her personal problems. She complained bitterly about Betty's father, saying that he had always wanted the child to accept his ways, regardless of her needs. At the same time, her own ambivalence about Betty became apparent. "I like a well-behaved child, BUT well-behaved!" she said emphatically. She complained about not being greeted affectionately by her daughter when she walked into the schoolyard, and felt that "please" and "thank you" should be forthcoming at the right times.

The teacher, confused by the contradictions and distortions of both parents, used this conference only to gain more information about Betty. She said little, but offered to meet with Betty's mother soon again.

Dissatisfied and angry with the teacher because she did not offer specific directives, the mother turned to the director of the school. "Things are different here than they were in the summer," she complained. "Betty is a loving child; she wants to be greeted warmly when she comes into school. How can you feel loving with a statue, like this teacher?" The director neither defended the teacher nor accepted the criticism, but instead made an appointment for a conference.

The director and teacher felt that it was time to re-evaluate the situation in terms of the mother's limitations and Betty's needs. Mrs. E's pressing personal difficulties, coupled with her need to blame others for her own failures, made it clear to them that counseling would be of little value. On the other hand, Betty had made some progress in school. Although she was still restless and without direction, she now stayed with her group and her teacher, and even had made some attempts to participate in activities. For Betty, school was surely the one stable element in her present life.

Both staff members tried to plan the next conference with all of this in mind. They decided that Betty's mother should be urged to seek professional help. Mrs. E. had indicated that she was troubled and needed a kind of guidance which, it was felt, was beyond the school's scope. However, anticipating the possibility of Mrs. E's rejecting our recommendations, we kept in mind that our aim would be to keep Betty, for her own benefit, in school whatever the response of the mother.

The teacher began the next conference by saying that Betty was doing better in school, but that she was still far from happy. She suggested that Betty might be reacting to her mother's own unhappiness over her marital rift. Mrs. E. readily agreed. The teacher then asked if Mrs. E. had thought about seeking professional help. "This is a difficult and lonely time for anyone and professional aid could be of great benefit at this time." Mrs. E. said that she had considered psychiatric help but that it was financially impossible. She then tried to place the blame for Betty's troubles on the school, on Betty's father, and on other areas which did not involve her. Unfortunately, Mrs. E. was not ready to follow the school's suggestion. The teacher and director, accepting her resistance, continued the conference by discussing some minor problems of Betty's. Mrs. E. left feeling reassured that the staff was friendly and wanted to help. But nevertheless the conference, in terms of its primary goal of parent guidance, had failed.

CHAPTER TWELVE

TECHNIQUES OF PARENT COUNSELING

Counseling of any kind is an art, a skill that cannot be learned from books alone. It is primarily developed and perfected through continuous experience in human relations and everyday living, supported by an ever-increasing body of knowledge along psychological, educational, and cultural lines. Techniques have been formulated, however, which reduce the trial and error of experience. These methods, when studied in the early years of teaching, are a valuable preparation; and when combined with simple counseling under careful supervision can provide the inexperienced teacher with a firm foundation.

PERSONAL QUALIFICATIONS

Since parent counseling deals primarily with emotions, there are certain prerequisites that anyone working in this field should strive to fulfill. In order to develop a professional attitude—friendly but objective, sympathetic yet uninvolved—the counselor should know herself. She should be able to recognize and admit her own prejudices and be aware of reasons for her behavior. She must be a good observer, a patient and detached listener.

AIMS OF COUNSELING

Parent counseling in the nursery school has as its general aim the education of the parent. Our goal is to support or influence parental attitudes and values through teaching.

TYPES OF CONFERENCES

There are three types of conferences, involving different objectives and techniques. First, the initial interview, the purpose of which is to gain information and insight into the nature of the child's personality and development. Since this is the only conference that takes place with little or no prior knowledge of the parent, it is also a means of establishing a relationship.

Second is the progress report—a regularly scheduled conference which gives the parent a reliable and well-rounded picture of her child in school. Because she feels that this is a routine procedure, the mother is generally at ease, and in response to the interest and attention given her child she will frequently bring up problems troublesome to her. This progress report is the best introduction to parent counseling for the young teacher.

The third group we call the "special problems" conference, initiated by parent or teacher for the purpose of discussing a particular problem of the child. Our models are illustrations of these typical problems brought to the nursery school staff.

PREPARATION

Before any conference the counselor must review her knowledge of the child and his mother by observing the child beforehand and re-examining all the recorded material.

OPENING THE CONFERENCE

At the start of a conference it is advisable that the parent be put at her ease. When the counselor herself is relaxed this is accomplished without too much difficulty. Some words of welcome, an indication of genuine interest in the child, and attention to the parent's comfort—all contribute to a good beginning. If the counselor opens with simple positive information about the child's adjustment and relationships in the nursery school situation, a parent feels, "She knows my child. I can trust her," and is generally ready to respond.

PROCEDURE

In an initial, history-taking interview it is usually necessary to record facts, such as: time of weaning, when toilet training was accomplished, etc. Note taking as a general practice, however, is inadvisable. It interferes with the necessary undivided attention required of the counselor, and with the spontaneity of the parent. It is important to record the conference soon after it has occurred, because memory is often unreliable. Over a period of time written records give chronological evidence of all changes in the child, and are an invaluable aid to the counselor.

In every case it is of primary importance that the counselor listen carefully to the mother's report, for usually she has sound intuitive understanding of her child. She has had an almost exclusive part in his gratifications, his frustrations, and his accomplishments. The counselor must respect this close-knit relationship, and hope to learn from the mother's insight and experience.

While the mother talks, the counselor must evaluate the material, selecting pertinent details to use in discussion. She will have opportunities to guide the conference through thoughtful answers to the mother's statements. She should redirect the course of the conference, when necessary, using tactful questions relating to the child's situation. This entire process is governed by two fundamental principles. First, all material must be related directly to the child and his immediate problem; and second, the material should be used so as to enlarge the mother's knowledge of childhood.

Guiding Precepts

In giving advice the counselor will try to use clear, concrete statements. She will avoid technical terms, and never overwhelm a parent by giving too much information.

The counselor will adroitly discourage remarks dealing

with marital friction, or any communication extraneous to her central concern—the sound development of the child.

She will attempt to keep the mother's negative feelings at a minimum, while avoiding overdependence. Because she is aware of the mother's tendency to react to her child's difficulties with feelings of personal involvement, she is careful to put her suggestions in a positive way. For the counselor knows she cannot educate without strengthening the mother's faith in herself.

The conference should not run over the allotted time— an hour at most. For longer conferences are exhausting to both parties.

LIMITATIONS TO COUNSELING

As there are many imponderables involved when dealing with human behavior, ready answers are not available. The counselor should not hesitate to admit her own inability to offer help in the solution of a particular problem, if such should be the case. She should, however, indicate her desire to give it further thought and look forward to a more fruitful conference in the future. No conference is a final statement. The young child is constantly growing and changing in a dynamic way. For this reason, no final answers can be given.

BIBLIOGRAPHY

The choice of the Bibliography has been confined to the literature concerning the developmental approach toward the young child in its formative years. It excludes the purely academic psychology and deals only with the child's emotional response to inner and outer forces which create predominantly his future personality. The order of sequence of the Bibliography is in accordance with the basic importance of the given literature.

Freud, Anna. *Psychoanalysis for Teachers and Parents.* New York: Emerson Books, 1935.

    Basic concepts of the child's development.

Balint, Alice. *The Early Years of Life.* New York: Basic Books, 1954.

    A psychoanalytic study of the child's development in his preschool age and a discussion of the problems of growing up.

Freud, Anna. "The Psychoanalytic Study of Infantile Feeding Disturbances." *The Psychoanalytic Study of the Child,* Vol. II. New York: International Universities Press, 1946.

    Normal feeding problems are put in contrast to pathological disturbances.

Freud, Anna and Burlingham, Dorothy. *Infants Without Families.* New York: International Universities Press, 1944.

    A comparison of the development of children under institutional care, based on the experience of the Hampstead Residential Nursery.

Freud, Anna and Burlingham, Dorothy. *War and Children*. New York: International Universities Press, 1943.

Authors describe the influence of war and bombing on the children's innate destructive drive. They discuss the problem of modification of infantile aggression in a hostile world of open disruption.

Parent Guidance Series. "Children's Fears," "Children's Jealousies," "Children's Temper Tantrums," "Breast Feeding," by Ruth Thomas. London: Family Health Publications, Maurice Craig House.

A valuable series about the child's instinct modifications.

Peller, Lili E. "Libidinal Phases, Ego Development and Play." *The Psychoanalytic Study of the Child*, Vol. IX. New York: International Universities Press, 1954.

Ridenour, Nina. *Some Special Problems of Children, Aged 2-5 Years*. New York: New York City Committee on Mental Hygiene, 1947.

Gruenberg, Sidonie M. *We, the Parents*. New York: Harper and Brothers, 1939.

An informal discussion of the joys and problems of parents and children living together in our modern world.

The
New & Updated
Copyright
Primer

A Survival Guide to Copyright
and the Permissions Process

Developed and written by the members of the
AAP Rights and Permissions Advisory Committee

aap
Association of American Publishers, Inc.

Additional copies may be obtained from:
Association of American Publishers, Inc.
50 F Street, NW
Washington, DC 20001
http://www.publishers.org

All appended materials, including sample letters, are samples intended to be used as general guidelines only.

CREDITS

With Special Thanks To:

* **AAP Rights and Permissions Advisory Committee**
* **Bonnie Beacher**, *The McGraw-Hill Companies*, New York, NY
* **Bill Hagen**, *IEEE*, Piscataway, NJ
* **Jon Baumgarten**, Esq., *Proskauer Rose LLP*, Washington, DC
* **Anne Reifsnyder**, *Aries/PS*, Somerset, NJ
* **Nisha Tyree** and **Carol Risher**, *Association of American Publishers*, Washington, DC

Contents

INTRODUCTION

Three years ago, the AAP Rights and Permissions Advisory Committee provided you with *The Copyright Primer: A Survival Guide to the Copyrights and Permissions Process* ("The Primer"). Since 1997, much has happened in the area of copyright law, rights, and licensing. It is for this reason that AAP felt it necessary to provide you with a revised edition of The Primer.

The purpose of the revised Primer is to provide a reference for anybody working in publishing or related industries in the area of rights or licensing. It remains a practical and theoretical manual that outlines the basic concepts of copyright law, copyright registrations and renewals; reversions of rights; permission licenses; and provides a brief outline of the principles of subsidiary rights licensing.

Highlights of this new edition include summaries of the Digital Millennium Copyright Act, the Sonny Bono Term Extension Act, amendments concerning exemptions for the blind, and the Copyright Office report on digital distance education.

We hope you will be able to use this book whenever you have a question arising from your daily work, from what copyright form to fill out for a CD-ROM, to whether a quote that an author wants to use in his book is in the public domain.

We trust that *The New and Updated Copyright Primer* will be a valuable resource for all publishing professionals, from copyright assistants to permission managers to editors, and to anyone else who has an interest in rights issues.

Chapter 1
U.S. COPYRIGHT LAW

*"The Congress shall have Power...To promote the Progress
of Science and useful Arts, by securing for limited Times to
Authors and Inventors the exclusive Right to their respective
Writings and Discoveries"*

— United States Constitution, Article 1, Section 8

A BRIEF HISTORY OF COPYRIGHT PROTECTION IN THE UNITED STATES

Copyrights are statutory grants of certain rights to authors and creators for a specified period of time to protect their "original" works.

Both published and unpublished works are protected under copyright law. The copyright owner retains certain exclusive rights, including: the right to reproduce the copyrighted work in any format; to prepare *derivative* works, including translations; to distribute copies to the public; and to perform and display the work publicly.

There have been three major revisions and a major amendment made to U.S. copyright law during the twentieth century: the Copyright Acts of 1909, 1976, 1989, and the Digital Millennium Copyright Act (1998). Work currently under copyright may be subject to the provisions of previous Copyright Acts.

The Copyright Act of 1909

The Copyright Act of 1909 took effect on March 4, 1909. It set a duration of protection at an initial term of 28 years, with a renewal term of an additional 28 years if the author/creator applied for extended protection before the expiration of the initial term.

Under the 1909 Act, most unpublished works were not protected by federal copyright law but by common law or state laws. An author's work was automatically protected by statute in most states as soon as the work was created, and as long as the work remained unpublished. Formal registration of a work terminated this common law protection. Once registered, a work—whether published or unpublished—was then protected under the federal statute. Registration in unpublished form was only possible for limited types of works. Publication also secured federal protection under the 1909 Act.

The formalities of copyright under the 1909 Act were very stringent. In particular, the 1909 Act stressed the importance of a copyright notice for securing copyright in published works. The statute contained specific provisions regarding the wording and location of the notice; an error in the copyright notice of a published work caused the work to enter the *public domain* (the copyright would be permanently lost and could not be restored or reclaimed). In addition, a work would lose *both* state common law and statutory protection if it was published without the proper copyright notice.

Under the 1909 Act, *publication* did not necessarily require the formality of placing a work on sale; the unrestricted sale or free distribution of one or more copies of a work to the public could constitute publication.

The Copyright Act of 1976

The 1976 Copyright Act took effect on January 1, 1978. It was designed to eliminate the difficulties of determining and enforcing authors' rights under a variety of state common laws. It provided for federal copyright protection upon creation.

Under this reform, works obtaining copyright protection after 1978 (created after 1977 or not published or federally registered in or before 1978) were granted protection for the life of the author plus 50 years, with no requirement of renewal. For *works-made-for-hire* and for *anonymous* and *pseudonymous* works, the term of copyright was set at 75 years from first publication or 100 years from creation, whichever expires first, again with no requirement for renewal.

For works published or registered prior to January 1, 1978, the new law preserved the dual copyright term established under the 1909 law. However, the renewal period was extended to 47 years for a maximum of 75 years (e.g., the original 28-year term plus a 47-year renewal term) for those works whose copyrights had not expired.

Under the 1976 Act, copyright registration is not necessary to secure federal statutory copyright protection. However, there are important commercial and legal benefits to registration (e.g., statutory damages and attorneys' fees). Furthermore, in order to initiate a copyright infringement action, the copyright must first be registered by American and foreign copyright owners.

In addition to eliminating the need for registration, the 1976 Act also relaxed the requirements regarding the copyright notice. It required that the notice be affixed to copies in "such manner and location as to give reasonable notice of the claim of copyright."[1]

It also eased the penalties for publishing a work with an incorrect copyright notice. Under the 1976 Act, omission of the notice on works published after 1978 did not automatically place the work in the public domain in certain instances. Such an error or omission did not invalidate the copyright in a work if:

- the notice was omitted from no more than a relatively small number of copies distributed to the public; or
- registration for the work was made before or within five years after publication without notice, and a reasonable effort was made to add notice to all copies that are distributed to the public in the U.S. after the omission was discovered; or
- the notice was omitted in violation of an express requirement in writing that, as a condition of the copyright owner's authorization of the public distribution of copies, they bear the prescribed notice.[2]

If the copyright owner's name or the date was missing from the notice or was incorrect, the work was considered to have been published without any notice. The 1989 Act relaxed the copyright notice requirements making notice purely voluntary, although it is still recommended for some legal, but mostly commercial, purposes.

The Berne Convention Implementation Act of 1989

On March 1, 1989, the United States became a member of the Berne Convention for the Protection of Literary and Artistic Works. The 1976 U.S. Copyright Act paved the way for the United States to join the Berne Convention by eliminating registration and by easing the notice require-

---

[1] Public law 94-553, Title 17—Copyrights, 405.

[2] Ibid.

ments as conditions for copyright protection, and by extending the term of protection. These changes were needed to bring the United States into compliance with the international norms outlined in Berne. The U.S. absence from the Berne Convention had diminished our position in the international market.

Under the Berne Convention, copyright protection may not be conditional on the observance of any formalities such as notice or registration. However, even Berne countries can impose formalities like registration or deposit on its own nationals or nationals of countries not members of Berne.

Duration of copyright protection for U.S. works in other countries party to the Berne Convention is essentially the same as in the U.S. Copyright Act.

Under the 1989 Act, as under the 1976 Act, registration of copyright is not mandatory for works that originated in the United States. However, for American and some foreign authors, registration is still required before a lawsuit can be brought for copyright infringement. Under the 1989 Act, registration provides prima facie evidence that the copyright is valid (in other words, an accused infringer must prove that the copyright is not valid rather than the copyright holder proving that it is) and that the facts stated on the registration certificate are valid. The act of registration also reaffirms the 1976 provision that only works registered before an infringement, or within three months of publication, may be eligible for awards of attorneys' fees and statutory damages.

Because the Berne Convention states that the enjoyment and exercise of rights should not be subject to any formality, the 1989 Act abolished mandatory notice of copyright for all works first published on or after March 1, 1989. However, it does allow a copyright notice to be placed on all distributed copies. Voluntary use of the notice is encouraged and it is widely used in the United States, since a notice of copyright will defeat a claim of innocent infringement relating to damages, in addition to providing vital information to those wishing to reprint a portion of the work.

Digital Millennium Copyright Act (DMCA)

On October 12, 1998, Congress passed the DMCA, legislation that makes changes in U.S. copyright law to address the digitally networked environment. The main purpose of the Act is to implement two World

Intellectual Property Organization (WIPO) treaties (see page 73) adopted in December 1996, which, when ratified by 30 nations, will effectively raise international standards of copyright protection to the levels of U.S. law and will establish the basis for their application in the digital environment.

There are six highlights of the DMCA that we feel are important to outline in this book:

I.   *Circumvention of Technological Measures:* The DMCA makes it illegal to manufacture or provide devices or services that circumvent encryption or other technological measures used to control access to copyrighted works, or to protect the rights of copyright owners in copyrighted works.

   Note: The effective date for the prohibition on the act of circumventing access controls is delayed for two years, until a rulemaking determines whether users of certain works are "adversely affected" by the prohibition in their ability to make non-infringing uses of them. (The prohibitions on providing devices that circumvent access and copy controls are not delayed.)

   Note: A device (or component of one) is illegal if it (1) is primarily designed or produced for the purpose of circumventing, (2) has only limited commercially significant use other than circumventing, or (3) is marketed for use in circumventing.

II. *Copyright Management Information (CMI):* The DMCA makes it illegal to knowingly alter, remove, or falsify CMI – or to knowingly traffick in copies of works linked with CMI that have been so altered, removed, or falsified – with an intent to enable or conceal copyright infringement.

III. *Enforcement:* The DMCA establishes civil and criminal penalties for violations of the prohibitions regarding circumvention and CMI.

IV. *Rights of Copyright Owners and Related Limitations:* The DMCA explicitly preserves, without modification, existing rights of copyright owners and the limitations on such rights, including fair use, in connection with

questions of copyright infringement. (But these limitations are not intended to apply to actions for circumvention; in that case, a specific set of limitations is provided.)

V. *Online Service Provider (OSP) Liability:* The DMCA clarifies
rules concerning liability of OSPs for copyright infringe-
ments occurring on their systems and networks.

There are four categories of OSP services outlined in
the DMCA: mere conduit, system caching, providing
access to materials posted by a user, and providing
information location tools.

The DMCA does not change existing law on what
constitutes an infringement (or a defense to an infringement), or existing legal doctrines under which a party
may be held responsible for infringing conduct by
another (except in limited cases with respect to universities and their faculty/graduate student employees).

The DMCA allows OSPs to avoid liability for monetary
damages and certain kinds of injunctive relief while
providing incentives for OSPs to "take-down" infringing material on their systems when they have knowledge, awareness, or notice of such material.

VI. *Concerns of Libraries and Educational Institutions:* The
DMCA addresses concerns of potential adverse effects
from the anti-circumvention provisions on these entities and other users of copyrighted works, without
legalizing a market in circumvention devices or creating
a fair use "right of access" to copyrighted works.

The DMCA updates current copyright law exemptions for library preservation and replacement of
copyrighted works by permitting limited use of digital
technologies (libraries can now preserve three (3)
copies and can replace copyrighted works that exist in
obsolete formats).

The DMCA provides for a study on "distance education" by the U.S. Copyright Office with a report to
Congress within six months of enactment. The report
was issued in May 1999.

CURRENT U.S. COPYRIGHT LAW

Copyright protects original works of authorship fixed in any tangible medium of expression, now known or later developed, from which they can be perceived, reproduced, or communicated either directly or with the aid of a machine or device.

There are two basic criteria as to what constitutes copyrightable matter:

- it must be an original work of authorship;
- it must be fixed in a tangible medium of expression for a period of more than transitory duration.

Copyrightable works include the following categories:

- literary works (including compilations);
- musical works, including any accompanying words;
- dramatic works, including any accompanying music;
- pantomimes and choreographic works;
- pictorial, graphic, and sculptural works;
- motion pictures and other audiovisual works;
- sound recordings;
- architectural works;
- computer programs, which are generally protected as literary works.

The copyrightable element in compilations and derivative works is of particular interest:

"A 'compilation' is a work formed by the collection and assembling of preexisting materials or of data that are selected, coordinated, or arranged in such a way that the resulting work as a whole constitutes an original work of authorship." *17 U.S.C. Section 101.*

Copyright in a compilation protects the selection or arrangement of the individual pieces in the compilation as well as any new text originally published therein.

Note: In terms of copyright, a "collective work" is a compilation of materials that separately constitute independent works, such as an anthology, encyclopedia, or periodical issue.

"A 'derivative work' is a work based on one or more preexisting works, such as a translation, musical arrangement, dramatization, fictionalization, motion picture version, sound recording, art reproduction, abridgment, condensation, or any other form in which a work may be recast, transformed, or adapted. A work consisting of editorial revisions, annotations, elaborations or other modifications which, as a whole, represent an original work of authorship, is a 'derivative work'." *17 U.S.C. Section 101.*

Several categories of material are generally not eligible for statutory copyright protection.[3] These include:

- works that have not been fixed in a tangible form of expression;
- titles, names, short phrases, and slogans; familiar symbols or designs; mere variations of typographic ornamentation, lettering, or coloring;
- mere listings of ingredients or contents;
- ideas, procedures, methods, systems, processes, concepts, principles, discoveries, or devices;
- works consisting entirely of information that is common property and containing no original authorship, i.e., standard calendars, height and weight charts, tape measures and rulers, and lists or tables taken from public documents or other public domain sources.

While facts themselves are not protected under copyright, the arrangement, selection, or compilation of facts may be considered a work of authorship.

Works that would normally be eligible for copyright protection but are not protected are said to be in the public domain. A work may be in the public domain in one country but still under copyright protection in others. Works enter the public domain in four basic ways:

- they were protected by copyright, but the copyright term has expired;
- they were eligible for copyright protection at the time of creation or publication but did not obtain protection because of a failure by the creator to properly fulfill all requirements for obtaining copyright protection under the then existing copyright laws;
- they were eligible for copyright protection, but the creator dedicated the work to the public domain (by forfeiture or abandonment);

---

[3] Several of these categories may, however, be protected under trademark and patent laws.

- they were prepared by a U.S. government official or employee, as part of that person's duties. The Copyright Act does not prevent copyright protection in works of state and local governments; however, the governmental bodies themselves may place the works in the public domain. Some states award exclusive contracts to be the "official" publisher of enhanced collections of state statutes, or of court decisions in official, copyrighted reporters – and public policy will forbid protection of individual state laws and similar edicts.

Ownership and Rights

The author of an original work is the owner of the work, except in cases where the work is a "work made for hire." The copyright law defines a work made for hire as one:

- created by an employee within the scope of his or her employment; or
- specially ordered or commissioned and fitting into one of nine categories of work: a contribution to a collective work; part of a motion picture or other audiovisual work; a translation; a supplementary work; a compilation; an instructional text; a test; answer material for a test; or an atlas; AND the parties expressly agree in a written instrument (signed by both parties) that the work shall be considered a work made for hire.

When a work is a work made for hire, the employer or other person for whom the work was prepared is considered the author under the copyright law and has all the exclusive rights of an author.

An author's exclusive rights under copyright are:

- the right to reproduce the work;
- the right to prepare derivative works based on the copyrighted work;
- the right to distribute copies of the copyrighted work to the public by sale or other transfer of ownership, or by rental, lease, or lending;
- the right to perform the copyrighted work publicly;
- the right to display the copyrighted work publicly.

Current U.S. copyright law provides for a number of limitations on these exclusive rights – two major exceptions are for certain limited uses which libraries may make of copyrighted material, and an exception allowing persons to use portions of copyrighted material under the concept of fair use.

Exceptions for Libraries

Under U.S. copyright law, libraries are able to make copies of some copyrighted materials in certain limited situations. The library must derive no commercial advantage, direct or indirect, in making the copy; the collection of the library must be open to the public; and the reproduction have a copyright notice (see "Commencement and Duration of Copyright" section for information about copyright notices). In addition to meeting these criteria, the reproduction must be for one of the following uses:

- to replace a damaged or lost copy;
- for use as a backup, security copy;
- at the request of a library patron for a copy of an excerpt from a work, but only if (1) the copy becomes the property of the patron; (2) the library has had no notice that the copy would be used for any purpose other than private study, scholarship, or research; and (3) the library displays a warning regarding illegal uses of copyrighted material on its request form and where orders for copies are accepted;
- at the request of a library patron for a copy of an entire work if the library determines that a copy of the work cannot be obtained at a fair price, AND conditions (1), (2), and (3) that appear in the previous bullet are met.

Fair Use Exceptions

U.S. copyright law also imposes some limitations on the exclusive rights owned by the copyright holder under the doctrine of fair use. Section 107 of the Copyright Act declares that certain uses of excerpts from a work for purposes such as comment, criticism, or study are "fair uses" for which the copyright owner's consent is not necessary.

The Copyright Act does not provide a precise definition of what constitutes fair use, but instead provides four factors which must be considered to determine whether any particular use is fair use. The four factors are:

- the purpose and character of the use, including whether such use is of a commercial nature or is for non-profit educational purposes;
- the nature of the copyrighted work;
- the amount and substantiality of the portion of the work used in relation to the copyrighted work as a whole; and
- the effect of the use in question upon the potential market for or value of the copyrighted work.

Each potential fair use situation is determined by its specific facts and all four factors must be considered. There are no numerical guidelines in copyright law which define how much, if any, material may be used under the fair use doctrine or any other specifics of the four factors. However, there are several sets of guidelines included in the legislative history of the various Copyright Acts (see below). And many publishing houses have suggested inhouse guidelines to help staff determine word counts for use of small excerpts.

Books and Periodicals. In 1976, the U.S. Congress endorsed fair use guidelines for educators making multiple copies of portions of books and periodicals for use in classrooms. The guidelines also permit educators to make single copies of lengthier portions. On the other hand, the guidelines expressly prohibit some types of copying as not being fair use, such as making unauthorized coursepacks, and court cases support this prohibition. These guidelines do not apply to computer software.

Television Programming. In 1981, a Congressional committee endorsed guidelines that permit individual educators to record broadcast television programming (but not pay-per-view) and to play the recording soon after the broadcast in the course of relevant teaching activities.

Educational Multimedia Presentations. In late 1996, a Congressional subcommittee recognized guidelines that permit educators and students to reproduce and adapt portions of books, movies, sound recordings, and computer program screen displays for use in educational multimedia presentations.

Distance Learning. During the May 1997 meeting of the Conference on Fair Use (CONFU), the Distance Learning and Image Archive

Guidelines did not achieve full support from proprietors and users alike. However, the academic community can consider them guidelines for print materials knowing that if they stay within the guidelines there is support for that behavior as fair use. Beyond the guidelines, consider the four fair use factors.

For more information about fair use and guidelines, ask the U.S. Copyright Office to send you "Circular 21 – Reproduction of Copyrighted Works by Educators and Librarians." The Copyright Office can be reached at 202-707-9100, and at http://www.loc.gov/copyright/circs.html. Multimedia and Distance Learning guidelines are reprinted in the Final Report of the Conference on Fair Use at http://www.uspto.gov.

Commencement and Duration of Copyright

The commencement and duration of copyright protection for a work depends on what copyright law was in effect at the time the work was originally created.

For works created prior to January 1, 1978, federal statutory copyright protection began upon publication of the work with a copyright notice OR registration of certain unpublished works. Unpublished works were otherwise protected by common law (in perpetuity). For works created on or after January 1, 1978, copyright protection begins from the moment an original work of authorship is created in fixed form (i.e., neither publication nor registration is necessary to obtain protection). However, for works published prior to March 1, 1989, a work must contain a copyright notice to avoid potential loss of copyright. Note that although registration is not required to obtain copyright protection, there are additional benefits from filing for registration (see page 21, "Copyright Registration Procedures" for a description of these benefits).

For purposes of copyright law, "publication" is the distribution of copies of a work to the public by sale or other transfer of ownership, or lease or lending, or the offering to distribute copies to a group of people for certain purposes. Although publication is no longer required to obtain copyright in an unregistered work, the concept of publication remains important for several reasons, including its application to works created prior to 1978.

As noted above, works published prior to March 1, 1989 must contain a copyright notice to avoid loss of copyright (refer to page 5 for exceptions). A proper copyright notice must include the following elements:

- the symbol "©" or the word "Copyright" or abbreviation "Copr.";
- the copyright year (year of first publication); and
- the name of the copyright owner.

Sonny Bono Copyright Term Extension Act of 1998

The main purpose of the Sonny Bono Copyright Term Extension Act is to extend basic terms of copyright protection under U.S. law by an additional 20 years to match the European Community's term of "life of the author + 70" years. It was named after the late entertainer/ Congressional Representative (R-CA) and enacted in October 1998.

Extension of Duration of Copyright: extends various terms, including for unpublished works, by an additional 20 years, but does not restore copyright protection to works that have already entered the public domain.

Termination Rights: provides limited revival of the termination right (other than in works for hire) for a work in its renewal term on the effective date of the Act (i.e., January 27, 1999), if the author or owner has not previously exercised the right. Specifies conditions for termination of transfer or license of renewal copyright executed before January 1, 1978. Also specifies that author's executor, administrator, personal representative, or trustee shall own the author's entire termination interest in the event author's widow/widower, children, and grandchildren are not living.

Use by Libraries and Archives: provides that, during the last 20 years of any term of copyright of a certain published work, such entity (including a non-profit educational institution that functions as such) may reproduce, distribute, display, or perform the work (including in digital form) for purposes of preservation, scholarship, or research – without permission of the copyright owner – unless, upon reasonable investigation, it determines that (1) the work is subject to normal commercial exploitation, (2) a copy or phonorecord of the work can be obtained at a reasonable price, or (3) pursuant to regulations issued by the Register of Copyrights, the copyright owner or its agent has provided notice that either of the other two conditions applies. (Providing such notice is entirely voluntary under the Act.)

Duration of Copyright

Generally, works fall into one of four categories:

- **Works originally copyrighted before 1950 and renewed before 1978:** These works have automatically been given a copyright term of 95 years (a first term of 28 years plus a renewal term of 67 years).

- **Works originally copyrighted between January 1, 1950 and December 31, 1963:** Copyrights in their first 28-year term on January 1, 1978 still had to be renewed in order to be protected for the second term. If a valid renewal was made at the proper time, the second term was 67 years. However, if renewal was not made, copyrights secured between 1950 and 1963 expired on December 31 of their 28th year.

- **Works originally copyrighted between January 1, 1964 and December 31, 1977:** The copyright law was amended on June 26, 1992 to make renewal optional. The copyright is still divided into a 28-year term and a 67-year renewal but if a formal renewal is not made, the renewal vests on behalf of the appropriate renewal claimant on December 31 of the 28th year.

- **Works originally created on and after January 1, 1978:** Generally, these works have a single copyright term of life of the author plus 70 years. In cases of a joint work, the term lasts for 70 years after the death of the last surviving author. For work for hire and anonymous and pseudonymous works, the term is 95 years from first publication or 120 years from creation, whichever is shorter.

Copyright Renewal

Copyright renewal terms only apply to works first created before January 1, 1978, as these works generally have a dual copyright term (the initial and renewal periods). Copyright in works created on or after that date have a single copyright term (the life of the author plus 70 years or fixed terms for works for hire and pseudonymous and anonymous works) and so are not subject to renewal requirements.

The Copyright Act of 1909 provided that a federal copyright could be secured for an original 28-year term and then renewed for an additional 28 years provided that a renewal registration was filed during the 28th year. Failure to make a timely renewal resulted in the permanent loss of copyright protection on the first day of the 29th year. The Copyright Act of 1976 extended the renewal term to 47 years for a total term of 75 years (that is, a 28-year original term and a 47-year renewal term). In 1998, this was extended by an additional 20 years (that is, a 67-year renewal term). The 1976 Act made no provision for restoring protection for works in which copyright had been lost for any reason. (A limited restoration provision was added in 1994 for certain *foreign* works that had entered the public domain in this country.) In 1992, the Copyright Law was amended to make renewal automatic for all works published on or after January 1, 1964. Thus, the copyright term for all works created between January 1, 1964, and December 31, 1977, are automatically renewed for the 67-year renewal period. However, a renewal registration may still be made, and whether renewal is automatic or made on application can affect the time the renewal vests and certain other matters.

The copyright law specifies that only the following persons may claim copyright in a renewal (except for certain categories of works listed below):

- the author, if living;
- the widow(er) and children of the author if the author is not living;
- the executor(s) of the author(s) estate if there is no surviving widow(er) or children; or
- the next of kin of the author if there is no will and if there is no surviving widow(er) or children.

There are certain types of works in which the owner of the copyright at the time of renewal registration may claim renewal:

- works made for hire;
- posthumous works; and
- periodical, cyclopedic, or other composite works.

In the case of derivative works, only the author of the new version of the work can be considered the author for renewal purposes. The author of the original work has no renewal rights in the new version of the work. However, the grant of the right to prepare derivative works in the renewal term may be terminated by the renewal rightsholder of the underlying original work.

When a copyright owner in the initial term grants rights in the original and the renewal term, the latter is effective only if the proper party (i.e., the renewal rightsholder) granted those rights. If the author of the work is the renewal owner, which is the case when the author survives into the renewal period, any agreement in which he agreed to transfer publishing rights or any of the other exclusive rights of copyright in the renewal term remains valid. However, if the author of a work dies before the 28th year of the original copyright term, rights to the work will belong to the renewal copyright owner(s) designated in the Copyright Act (as listed above) during the renewal term, regardless of any contractual commitments or assignments the author may have made to the contrary (for instance, a publishing agreement). Therefore, it is imperative for a publisher to identify the proper renewal claimant(s) and obtain any additional assignment(s) needed to allow continued publication and licensing of a work entering its renewal term even if that means buying rights from the author AND the widow(er) and other potential claimants.

The original copyright notice remains on a renewed work, but a reference to the renewal may be added; for example, "© 1952 by General Publishing House, Inc. Renewed 1980 by John Doe."

Transfer of Rights

A transfer of any exclusive rights under copyright, including the right to publish copies or to distribute or sell the work, must be in writing and signed by the author to be enforceable. Assignments and other transfer documents may be recorded in the U.S. Copyright Office. Recordation provides certain legal advantages to the transferee.

Termination of Grant of Rights

The Copyright Act provides the author or certain successors the right to terminate any grant of rights under U.S. copyright law (such as those provided in a publishing agreement) at the end of a specified number of years. The number of years depends upon the copyright law under which the grant was executed:

- **Works created before January 1, 1978.** Works created before January 1, 1978, are eligible for a renewal copyright term as noted above. If a clear assignment or grant of renewal rights was not made, the author can terminate use of the work in the renewal term. In addition, copyright law provides the author or certain successors the right to terminate any grant of rights in such works under United States copyright law at the end of the 28th year of the renewal term (e.g., the 56th year of the total copyright term), notwithstanding contractual obligations to the contrary, thereby reverting rights to the author or successor during the remaining years of the copyright term.

- **Grants executed on or after January 1, 1978.** For grants that do not include the right to publish, the author or successor may terminate the grant during a five-year period beginning 35 years from the date of the grant. For grants that do include the right to publish, the five-year period begins either 40 years from the date of the grant or 35 years from the date of publication of the work under the grant, whichever is earlier.

- The 1998 term extension legislation provides for a limited revival of termination rights (other than in works for hire) for a work subsisting in its renewal term on the effective date of that legislation (i.e., January 27, 1999). It also specifies that the author's executor, administrator, personal representative, or trustees would own the author's entire termination interest in the event that the author's widow or widower, children, and grandchildren are not living.

A derivative work prepared under authority of a grant before its termination may continue to be utilized, although no new derivative works based on the original work may be created. Finally (although not tested by court cases), termination is probably only applicable to domestic (i.e., U.S.) rights.

No Electronic Theft (NET) Act

The NET Act (enacted in December 1997) was intended to close a loophole in the Copyright Act in order to tighten criminal copyright infringement provisions.

The passage of the NET Act was in response to a decision in *United States v. LaMacchia*, where a loophole prevented the prosecution of an MIT student who created and operated an electronic bulletin board on the

Internet and solicited users to post and download copies of commercial copyrighted software. Although the illegal copying that occurred resulted in estimated losses in excess of $1 million to copyright owners, the charges against LaMacchia were dismissed because he did not financially gain from the endeavor and, in the absence of such a commercial motive, he could not be prosecuted for criminal infringement under the Copyright Act.

The NET Act:

- amended the definition of "financial gain" in the Copyright Act to include "anything of value";
- amended Section 506(a) of the Copyright Act to criminalize "willful infringement" – including by electronic means – causing more than $1,000 in damages in any 180-day period, even if acts are *not* for commercial advantage or private financial gain;
- clarified the "willfulness" standard by stating that "evidence of reproduction or distribution of a copyrighted work, by itself, shall not be sufficient to establish willful infringement";
- required the United States Sentencing Commission to implement sentencing guidelines "sufficiently stringent to deter such a crime," and "provide for consideration of the retail value and quantity of the items."

Digital Theft Deterrence and Copyright Improvement Act of 1999

On December 9, 1999, President Clinton signed the Digital Theft Deterrence and Copyright Improvement Act of 1999. The new law increases by 50 percent the statutory penalties for copyright infringement. It also facilitates prosecution of online piracy cases under the No Electronic Theft Act of 1997.

Chapter 2
COPYRIGHT REGISTRATION PROCEDURES

WHY REGISTER?

To obtain statutory damages. Registration must be made before an infringement occurs or within three months after publication in order to obtain statutory damages and attorney's fees (*17 U.S.C. Section 412*).

For evidentiary weight. Certificates of registrations made within five years of publication constitute *prima facie* evidence both of the validity of the copyright and the facts stated in the certificate (*17 U.S.C. Section 410(c)*).

For constructive notice. Documents recorded in the Copyright Office are given constructive notice of the facts stated in the recorded document, only if registration has been made for the work to which the document pertains. Documents of transfer can be accorded priority over a conflicting transfer based on the one executed first if the document has been timely recorded at the Copyright Office (*17 U.S.C. Section 205*).

To institute an infringement suit. All works of American origin and some foreign works must be registered before an action for copyright infringement can commence (*17 U.S.C. Section 411(a)*).

To cure omission of notice. An omission of notice from copies of a work published between 1978 and March 1, 1989 did not invalidate the copyright if the work was registered within five years and a reasonable effort was made to add the notice to copies publicly distributed in the United States (*17 U.S.C. Section 405*).

For commercial reasons. Licensing, collecting royalties, customs transactions, and other business dealings may require a registration certificate. Also, the Copyright Office's registration and recordation databases are on-line (and available via the Internet) for all post-1977 filings.

HOW TO APPLY FOR REGISTRATION

Application for copyright registration is made on the forms prescribed by the U.S. Copyright Office.

Under Section 408 of the Copyright Act, copyright registration of both published and unpublished works requires a registration form, a fee, and deposit of a copy (or copies for published works), phonorecord, or other material to identify the work for which registration is sought. The deposit serves as a record of the material that is registered, and permits a determination of copyrightability.

The Forms

A completed and signed registration form (one application per copyright claim) must accompany a filing for copyright registration. The following forms are available through the U.S. Copyright Office:

TX (for all nondramatic literary works, including computer programs);
VA (for artwork, photographs, board games);
PA (for multimedia works, videodiscs, motion pictures);
SR (for audio cassettes, sound recordings);
SE (for periodicals and serials).

For additional information: http://www.loc.gov/copyright.

Preparing the TX/VA/PA forms

The information needed for the TX, VA, and PA forms is basically the same. The information needed for most of the sections is clear, but some sections require some additional explanation.

Space 2: Name of Author. In cases where the work being registered is a subsequent edition or version of another work, only material that is new to the work being registered is covered by the registration. Accordingly, only authors who created new material for this version of the work should be listed on the certificate.

When the work qualifies as a work made for hire, the name of the author should be listed as the employer (usually the publisher) (see page 11 for the definition of a work made for hire). If the publisher owns all U.S. rights but it is not a work-for-hire, identify the author in Space 2 and the publisher as "claimant" in Space 4, noting in the transfer space how the publisher acquired rights (i.e., "by written agreement").

Space 2: Nature of Authorship. The "Nature of Authorship" section must indicate what material this author created for this edition of the work being registered. When there is more than one author for a work, the "Nature of Authorship" section should note this with language such as "author of Chapters 1–5" or "co-author of entire work."

When the work is a revision or new edition of a previous work, the "Nature of Authorship" section should also note this with language such as "foreword and introduction," or "revisions and new text." (In such cases, this section should agree with Space 6b, "Material Added to This Work"; see below.)

Space 6a: Preexisting Material. This section must be completed if the work being registered is a derivative work or compilation. Derivative works include subsequent editions or revisions of works, translations of works, and adaptations to other forms, such as a film version of a book. This section should note this with language such as "previous edition," "revision of...," "previous English version titled." Compilations include works that contain extensive material from other sources, such as anthologies or works with numerous excerpts, figures, or photos from other sources; this should be noted with language such as "compilation of previously published material" or "contains text and figures from other sources."

Space 6b: Material Added to This Work. This section must be filled in only for compilations. This and the previous section complement each other; while the first identifies the material that came from other sources, this section identifies the new material. This section should identify all material created by each author as listed in section 2; similar language should be used.

Errors or omissions in the copyright registration certificate can be corrected or amended by filing a CA form, although the presumptive effect of these changes is unclear. The information provided in the CA form supplements the information provided in the initial registration; it does not supersede it.

Effective January 1996, the U.S. Copyright Office now offers a short version of its application forms for any living author who is the only author and sole owner of the copyright. The information requested is minimal and the instructions are brief and to the point. Because the application must be signed by the author, not a representative of the author, it is not that useful for a large publisher to use these forms.

Preparing the RE renewal form

Most of the information needed to complete the RE (renewal) form is taken directly from the original registration form for the work being renewed. However, the renewal claimant (Section 1) will frequently be different from the copyright claimant on the original registration. Under U.S. copyright law, the renewal claimant must be one of the parties listed in the copyright statute (see page 17). If the original claimant was not the author (for instance, the publisher is often the copyright claimant as the owner of copyright), or if the author is deceased, the renewal claimant will be different from the original copyright claimant. To complete the RE form, the proper renewal claimant must be determined, based on whether the author is alive and what surviving statutory heirs there are under the copyright law.

When completing the renewal form, a publisher should also consider whether it will continue to own rights to the work in question during the renewal period if the author is deceased (see page 18). If it appears that rights will vest in the renewal claimant and not the publisher, the publisher may wish to enter into a new contractual arrangement with the renewal claimant, which will allow the publisher to continue to publish the work during the renewal period.

An application form may be submitted by the author, the copyright claimant if different from the author, the owner of exclusive rights in the work, or the authorized agent of the author.

The Fees¹ and Mailing Instructions

The prescribed, non-refundable fee (currently $30 per application).

Mail the signed and completed application form, two deposit copies (or one if unpublished), and the fee in the same envelope to:

Register of Copyrights
Copyright Office
Library of Congress
Washington, D.C. 20559-6000

Within about 16 weeks of the application's submission, the Copyright

---

¹ The fees cited here are correct as of the printing of this book. Check with the U.S. Copyright Office (http://www.loc.gov/copyright) for updates.

Office will send the publisher a certificate of registration to indicate the work has been registered. No acknowledgment is made by the Copyright Office when the application is received, although a certified mail receipt, or if hand-delivered a stamped receipt of delivery, can be obtained. If further information is needed, a Copyright Office Examiner will inquire by letter or telephone call. If an application is rejected, the copies of the work submitted under the mandatory deposit requirement will not be returned.

The Copyright Office does not provide free information on applications that have been submitted within the previous 16 weeks. If information on the status of a registration is needed prior to that time, contact the Certifications and Documents Section (202-707-6787), which can provide this information upon payment of applicable fees ($65/hour for an "in-process" search).

A copyright registration is effective on the date that all the required elements (application, fee, and deposit copies) in acceptable form are received in the Copyright Office, regardless of the length of time it takes the Copyright Office to process the application and mail the certificate of registration. A certificate is not required prior to publication or production of a work.

In all correspondence with the Copyright Office, publishers should include a contact name, a daytime telephone number, and their full address, including zip code. Be sure to send the non-refundable filing fee, the completed application form, and the non-refundable deposit in the same package. If desired, a cover letter explaining any instructions to the Copyright Office or assisting them with the application can be added, but remember that it becomes part of the public record, so do not include any confidential information or instructions.

Special or expedited handling

This is an important service provided by the Copyright Office when a work must be registered in order to file a claim for infringement or to meet a contractual (time) obligation. The fee for special handling is currently $530 per claim, and the Office promises a registration and issuance of a certificate in 5-7 business days.

The Deposit Copies

Books: Two complete copies of the work. The hardcover edition (not the paperback edition) is considered to be the "best" edition for deposit purposes. If a work is only available in electronic form, that is considered the best edition. Best edition requirements are spelled out in Circular 7b. For unpublished works or works first published outside the United States, only one deposit copy is required.

Software: The copyright law defines a computer program as a set of statements or instructions to be used directly or indirectly in a computer in order to bring about a certain result. Copyright protection does not extend to ideas, program logic, algorithms, systems, methods of operation, concepts, principles, or discoveries, regardless of the form in which it is described, explained, illustrated, or embodied in such work.

The deposit requirements for both published and unpublished computer programs are the source code for the entire program, if it is 50 pages or less. For longer programs, the requirement is the first and last 25 pages of source code, along with printed documentation such as user's manuals, guides, etc., if applicable. The program should be submitted in source code and reproduced in a form visually perceptible without the aid of a machine or device. The page or document containing the title of the work must also be included. If a program contains trade secret material, a claimant can submit the first and last 10 pages of the program, or the first and last 25 pages with portions (up to 49%) containing trade secrets blocked out (using black stripes or redacting). For more information, see Circular 61.

Where an applicant is unable or unwilling to deposit source code, object code may be deposited instead and the applicant must state in writing that the work as deposited in object code contains copyrightable material. The Copyright Office will send a letter stating that registration has been made under its "rule of doubt" and warning that it has not determined the existence of copyrightable material. This may affect the evidentiary benefits of registration.

CD-ROMs: The deposit requirements for CD-ROMs are a complete CD-ROM package including all accompanying software and manuals, plus a printed version of the work, if available.

Laser Discs: The deposit requirements for laser discs are one copy of the complete package plus a printed version of the work, either a videotape or photocopies of the complete laser contents.

Databases: A database may be either a "single-file database" or a "multiple-file database." The data records in a single-file database pertain to a single common subject matter, while a multiple-file database has separate and distinct groups of data records. Copyright does not protect facts and data. However, if there is sufficient authorship in the selection coordination or arrangement of information, including facts and data, there is copyright protection for that selection/arrangement as a compilation. Such a database can be registered with the Copyright Office.

If the author created categories or fields and arranged them in a particular order, copyright can be claimed in the "compilation of database information." Many databases have a computer program that accesses the database. If the database and content are created together or published together, the publisher may register both on a single application, that is, the program and the database compilation.

Even if the content of a database consists exclusively of previously published material, a publisher who has compiled this material in a sufficiently original way, may claim copyright in the arrangement of the content. If the database includes both new and old data, the publisher may register the additional (new) data as a compilation including any revised data, updates, and so forth.

The deposit requirements for a single-file database other than in CD-ROM format are a printout of the first and last 25 data records and the page containing the title of the work.

The deposit requirements for a multiple-file database other than in CD-ROM format are a printout of 50 pages or data records from each file, or the entire file, whichever is less (the Copyright Office would also prefer that this include a sample of any copyright notice affixed to the copies or container for the database); and a descriptive statement that includes the name and content of each separate file in the database, including subject matter, origin of data, and number of separate records in each file, and a description of the exact contents of any machine-readable copyright notice used in the database (including manner of use and frequency of display) and a sample of any visually perceptible copyright notice affixed to copies of the database.

The deposit requirements for a revised database including updates, revisions, etc. (either single-file or multiple-file) are a printout of 50 pages or data records showing the revisions, or the entire revised portions if less than 50 pages, and the pages containing the title of the work.

For databases published in CD-ROM format, the publisher must also deposit one complete copy of the CD-ROM in addition to the source code.

Note: The deposit requirements vary according to the type of work being registered. Be sure to refer to the instructions on the form before completing the application. For more information on the deposit requirements for multimedia works, see Circular 55; for motion pictures and video recordings, see Circular 45; for computer software programs, see Circular 61; for sound recordings, see Circular 56. When in doubt about which form to use or what to claim, call the Copyright Office for assistance at 202-707-3000. The registration of computer software and multimedia works can be very complicated, and often will require considerable investigation into the contract arrangements for each claim of authorship.

Note: Separate copyright claims for individual authors to the work (such as for text and art) often will appear on the copyright page or packaging of a work. The deposit requirement for Form TX is satisfied for all claims to copyright provided all applications are submitted together with the deposit copies of the work assuming the remitter of the copyright application owns all of the rights or is able to act as an agent for the owner(s) for registration purposes.

Mandatory deposit requirements

Section 407(a) of the Copyright Act requires a mandatory deposit in the Library of Congress, within three months of publication in the United States, of two complete copies of the best edition of a work for all works published in the United States. Submission of two copies of the best edition of a published work for registration satisfies this requirement. These works go through a selection process, whereby the Library of Congress may add them to its collections or use them in exchanges with other libraries, in order to add other works including foreign published materials to the Library of Congress collections. A long list of exempted works from the mandatory deposit requirements are identified in 407(c). Satisfying the mandatory deposit requirements alone does not provide the benefits of copyright registration but copyright registration does satisfy the mandatory deposit requirements. For CD-ROMs, the Library of Congress in a private contractual agreement has waived the requirement of deposit of two copies in exchange for the deposit of one copy and an agreed-upon license that specifies how the Library can use the CD-ROM. Copies of the permission license are available from the Library.

Special relief

The Copyright Office will consider an exception to the basic deposit requirements and will accept a deposit of identifying material instead of copies if no copies are available, or for secured tests, or one copy in lieu of two or a less than "best edition" all on a case-by-case basis. Requests for special relief must be made in writing and should accompany the registration application, fee, and deposit copies. If such a request is made *after* a registration has commenced, be sure to contact the Office and get a "control number" for the pending registration and include it prominently in the special relief (or special handling) request. Address the letter to:

Chief, Examining Division
U.S. Copyright Office
Library of Congress
Washington, DC 20559

USEFUL FACTS

To speed up your claims through the examination process, or if you have any doubt about what to deposit, what application form to use, or how to describe your authorship, call the Examining Division before submitting your claim.

- Examining Division: 202-707-8250
- Information Specialist: 202-707-5959 or 202-707-3000
- 24-Hour Copyright Hotline for forms and circulars: 202-707-9100.
- Copyright Office circulars also are available by fax: 202-707-2600 from any touch-tone telephone.

Frequently requested Copyright Office circulars and announcements are now available over the Internet at http://www.loc.gov/copyright.

Publishers may copy all U.S. Copyright Office circulars and informational materials without requesting permission. Blank application forms can be photocopied and used to submit registration applications; however, photocopied forms must be clear, legible, and on a good grade of 8½ inch by 11 inch white paper, suitable for automatic feeding through a copier and in the same two-sided format as original applications. The forms should be printed, preferably in black ink, head to head (so that the top of page two is directly behind the top of page one). Forms not meeting these requirements will be returned. You should allow two to three weeks for delivery of all ordered materials.

Copyright searches are performed by the U.S. Copyright Office (202-707-6850) for $65/hour. You can also search the Copyright Office database of registrations and renewals filed after 1977 and documents recorded after 1977. The database is accessed through the Copyright Office web page (see above for URL) and contains instructions for use.

A Guide to Which Application Form to Use for Nonprint Products

The following are examples of typical multimedia deposits showing the appropriate form and authorship statements for registration. The fact situations pertaining to a particular claim will determine the correct way to complete the form.

Form to Use	Nature of Deposit	Suggested Nature of Authorship Statement
PA	Slides and booklet	(1) Entire work or (2) Text and photography
PA	Slides (or filmstrips), booklet, and audiocassettes	(1) Entire work or (2) Text as printed and recorded, photography, and sounds
PA	Videocassette, manual with text and pictorial illustrations	(1) Entire work or (2) Cinematography, text and illustrations
PA	Filmstrip, pamphlets, poster, and music soundsheet	(1) Entire work or (2) Photography, text, artwork, lyrics, music, and sounds
PA	Manuals, containing artwork, and identifying materials (computer program listing, videotape) for machine-readable diskette that produces pictorial screen display	Printed text and artwork, text of computer program, and audiovisual work
PA	Manual, interactive compact disk, and identifying material for computer program on machine-readable diskette (or cassette)	Printed text, photographs, and text of computer program
SR	Audiocassettes and manual	**Do Not Use the Term "Entire Work" on Form SR** Text as printed and recorded, and sound recording
SR	Music soundsheets, booklets, and posters	Text, artwork, lyrics, music, and sound recording
SR	Audiocassettes, manual, and identifying material for computer program on machine-readable diskette (or cassette)	Text of manual and computer program, recorded text, and sound recording
TX	Manuals and identifying material for computer program on machine-readable diskette (or cassette), which produces textual screen display	Text of manuals and computer program

Chapter 3
PERMISSION LICENSES

SEEKING PERMISSION

In order to use the works of others, you need to apply for permission, unless the use can be considered a fair use or the work is in the *public domain* (use of the material is the exclusive right of the copyright holder under U.S. and foreign copyright laws). Permission must be obtained to photocopy excerpts or whole works to be used in course packs or posting on web sites or often as class handouts for educational purposes, just as permission is needed to republish in another publication. The first step in obtaining permission is to determine who controls the rights for the material being requested. The grantor may be a publisher, a literary agent, or an author/illustrator. An examination of the copyright page (usually the reverse of the title page in books, the masthead in journals) will provide some helpful information about where to send permissions requests. The publisher can usually grant permission, but rights are sometimes administered by an author or author's agent. Publishers typically control permissions for scientific and scholarly books and journals, and for most in-print trade books. For some in-print and most out-of-print trade books, and for articles in general circulation magazines, rights are often held by the authors.

Identifying the Primary Source

Identifying the primary source is most important and will save time when applying for permission. If the material was previously published or appears by permission, you will find a corresponding acknowledgment or credit line. Acknowledgments can be found in several places: below an illustration or excerpt, on the copyright page, in a separate acknowledgments section, or with the bibliographical references. A standard credit line includes author, title, publisher, copyright notice, and the words, "reprinted by permission," for example:

From *The History of Copyright in the United States* by John Smith. Copyright © 1994 by John Smith. Reprinted by permission of Scholarly Books Press.

Apply directly to the grantor of permission noted in the credit line. In this case, you would contact Scholarly Books Press for permission.

The Request Letter

The next step in obtaining permission is to prepare a request letter. A request should be specific and provide the grantor with information about the use to be made, including details about the new work, and identify the requested material.

Grantors will want the following information about the new publication:

1.   Title, author, and publisher
2.   Publication date
3.   Edition—text or trade and/or volume number
4.   Binding—hardcover or softcover
5.   Number of pages
6.   Proposed selling price
7.   Market—territory of distribution (for example, U.S. and Canada, or World)
8.   Language(s)
9.   Media formats
10. Quantity of first printing
11. Include information on distribution if the process includes scanning, digitizing, or other methods that require electronic rights
12. If rights to provide digital copies for the blind or print-disabled are needed.

List all supplementary items that will include the requested material: teachers' editions, instructors' manuals, transparencies, and so on. Whenever possible, include all requests for material from one publisher in one letter per project. Some grantors prefer not to issue separate contracts. When writing for permission for material that was used in a previous edition, it is helpful to include a copy of the previous grant of permission. Also, a request letter may include a place for the grantor's signature, indicating that permission has been granted. However, most publishers will reply with a contract containing specific terms of their own.

Permission requests are usually for *nonexclusive rights.* Acquiring exclusive rights requires a written transfer of rights and limits anyone else from using the work. You may want to request a permission that would extend to subsequent editions of your work. However, permission agreements are often restricted to one-time use only, or cover subsequent editions only where content changes are less than a specified percentage of the original work.

To ensure a timely reply when requesting permission, clearly identify the material being requested. If possible, send a copy of the selection and a complete description of the material you wish to use. Incomplete requests may be returned and will delay the granting process. Identify the title, author, page numbers, chapter title, volume and issue date for journals, and figure or table numbers. Also, *check to see if there is copyrighted material from another source within the selection requested,* such as a map, picture, illustration, or graph. A separate request for permission to quote that material must be sent; you may need to contact several publishers for permission to reprint one article.

If the material is being edited, adapted, or abridged in any way, the grantor must be informed. When making substantial changes, be sure to include a copy of the original selection with revisions and deletions clearly marked. Be prepared—authors and creators are protective of their work and some will not permit any modifications. When reprinting illustrations, particularly from children's books, you will find that many grantors have specific rules on how the art may be presented. Re-illustration is sometimes denied, and often any alterations (cropping, airbrushing, etc.) require that the new layout be submitted for approval.

Allow sufficient time to clear permissions. Response times vary; you may receive a quick reply or the wait may be six to eight weeks. The length of time for a response depends on several factors: extensive research may be needed in order for the publisher to process the request, ownership of rights might be unclear, additional editorial or author's approval may be necessary, or the permissions department may be experiencing a heavy volume of requests.

If a response is not received, try calling the grantor or sending a letter or fax marked "second request." The original request may have been misdirected. In some cases, the publisher no longer controls the rights or the work is out of print and rights have reverted to the author. In these cases, the request may have been forwarded to the author for granting. If you are not notified with a response to the request, *you cannot assume that the permission has been granted.*

Some grantors restrict the amount of material you can reprint. There may be restrictions placed on the total number of figures, tables, or excerpts used from any one work. Also, grantors may want to limit the number of times a particular selection appears in other works. A royalty arrangement may be required if a substantial amount of material is used from the works of one publisher. Requests for old, outdated material may be denied when a current edition of the work is available.

Use of Figures and Tables

Figures and tables usually need permission to be reprinted or redrawn, except if created from public domain documents and sources. Note that some government publications make use of tables and figures that are under copyright and do need permission.

Look for credit lines immediately below figures and tables and also for corresponding credits in acknowledgment sections. Some figures and tables are noted, "reprinted by permission" while others are cited only with credit to the source. Words or phrases such as *from, adapted from,* and *data from* in a source citation describe how a figure or table is compiled. *From* and *adapted from* indicate the selection is either used as it originally appeared or was adapted from the original, and so permission is needed. However, *data from* suggests that facts were used from a particular source in the new work but that permission may not have been obtained because the data used was not per se protectable.

Often multiple sources are noted, implying that the author has created a new compilation of data by virtue of selection or arrangement of it and permission would be needed for use of the new arrangement.

Redrawing someone else's art will not necessarily excuse you from obtaining permission. The term *redrawing* is sometimes applied to adapting the original work, but it is also used to describe a new rendering of a figure or creating a new piece of art from an existing one. If a figure is revised slightly (color added, labels altered, layout changed), it is still considered an adaptation or a derivative of the original and permission should be sought. However, if an existing figure is cast into a new form and a new expression is created from the data, permission may not be necessary. Even if no permission is required, you should supply proper acknowledgment in the form of a source note.

A table or figure is a unique entity (copyrightable "work") and is considered separate from any accompanying text when making a "fair use" determination. However, depending on the use and amount of information taken, a few entries from a table or data from a figure may in certain circumstances qualify as a "fair use."

Requesting Art

Permission is needed to reproduce all artwork, photographs, and advertisements from copyrighted publications. Rights are usually held by the photographer or a photographic agency. Also, a model release must be obtained from each person appearing in a photograph if the picture is not of a public scene or if it was taken in a controlled situation. Agencies supplying prints usually have secured the required releases, but it is best to verify this when requesting permission. Advertisements may contain logos, and approval may be needed from the ad agency and the sponsoring company. With fine art, museums and art galleries often control reproduction rights that govern usage.

Unpublished Works

Be extremely careful when quoting from unpublished works – private letters, theses, and so on. Permission should be requested for a quotation of any length from unpublished sources. For letters, permission is needed from the author, not the recipient, since the latter owns no reproduction rights. When requesting permission to use a "letter to the editor," contact the publisher of the journal or paper in which it appears. The publisher may have the right to grant, but usually you will be directed to obtain permission from the author of the letter. Student essays also require obtaining clearances, and if the student is a minor, a parent or legal guardian must also consent to the usage.

Paraphrasing

It is not a copyright infringement to read a factual or informational article and then write what was learned in one's own words without seeking permission. However, this is quite different from writing a piece by rearranging words and copying the expression, or the organization and sequence of the material. Excessive paraphrasing may be beyond the scope of "fair use" and may require seeking permission. Paraphrasing should not be used as a way of trying to circumvent the permissions process.

Receiving the Permission

Carefully examine the reply and take any action necessary to complete the negotiation. For instance, a grantor may ask you to sign and return a copy of the agreement for countersignature. Permission may be contingent upon securing the author's permission. A request may be denied solely because the copyright holder *does* have the right to refuse a request for permission. If a request is denied, you may want to find the reason for refusal; an accommodation may be reached.

Check to see if rights were granted for the requested territory. The publisher may not control rights to all the territory targeted for distribution. For example, a U.S. publisher may not be able to grant permission for Canadian rights. The publisher often will then direct you to the appropriate grantor for that territory.

A grant may specify a *reprint fee*, which may have to be paid before publication. Not all fees are flat; some grants include continuing royalty arrangements and ask for an advance against a set royalty rate. Some fees are based on a per-page rate or a per-line rate (prevalent in poetry reprints). Often the stature of the author and the popularity of the property determine the reprint fee.

Generally, contracts include the exact form of credit to be used. Some even impose penalties for using improper credit. Most grants have specific directives concerning placement of acknowledgments. They may require credit to appear on the same page as the selection or immediately below a figure or table. However, most ask that the notice be placed on the copyright page or in an acknowledgments section. If the grantor does not specify, the recommended form of acknowledgment is to cite: author, title, publisher, copyright notice, and "reprinted by permission."

Agreements may contain termination clauses that limit the use of the copyrighted material to a particular amount of time; 5- , 7- , or 10-year terms are common. After this period expires, a renewal of the license must be negotiated. You may be required to send the grantor a few complimentary copies of the new work upon publication. This enables the grantor to review the work, check for proper acknowledgment, and to see that the requirements governing the use of adaptations were executed.

SEEKING PERMISSION IN TRADE PUBLISHING

Clearing rights for material to be used in trade publications can be simple or extremely complicated, depending on the nature of the work. Novels, for instance, are often relatively easy, with only one or two pieces of material needing permission. A substantial biography, however, may require rights for hundreds of unpublished letters, photographs, magazine and newspaper articles, and various other items, depending on the nature and scope of the work.

The type of material needed, and its placement in the new work, will determine the complexity of obtaining permission to use it. Unlike college products, most trade publications consist of only one edition (the exception being reference titles), and there is not the same array of supplementary works accompanying the primary publication. The request letter, therefore, can be quite straightforward, specifying the rights needed, as well as the territory and language in which the publication will be distributed. Also, if there is potential to *sublicense* the work, it is worth trying to clear these rights at the same time. It will often facilitate permissions if requests include rights to grant use of the material to services producing products for the print and hearing disabled.

The issue of *fair use* is important in seeking rights for trade publications. *Never* assume fair use, no matter what the amount of material. Two lines of poetry, a song lyric, or a quote may not seem like much, but the copyright holders of this material may not interpret *any* use of the material as fair. Also, use of two lines of text from a novel or memoir may seem fair, but if it is to be used as an epigraph to set the tone for the new work, it may not fall under the fair use provisions. When using material from letters or other unpublished documents, very little is considered fair, no matter how seemingly insubstantial the material is in question. If there is any doubt, it is always worth seeking permission; in the use of unpublished works, it should be automatic.

It is best to start seeking permissions as early as possible because the process can be time consuming, for the following factors. Copyright holders of material commonly used in trade works evaluate these requests closely, and they sometimes must consult or seek approval from the author/illustrator, the author's agent, or the author's estate. Approval often involves more than just seeing if the rights are controlled and setting a fee. It is not unusual for the copyright holder to want to see exactly how the material is being used, including its exact placement in the work and what will surround it. Do not be surprised if editorial changes are required by the copyright holder as a condition to granting use. Many copyright holders are often less concerned with making money on the reuse than with losing control of the material. If rights are being sought for a commercial electronic use, expect extremely close scrutiny of the request and a very *narrow grant*, if any at all. In situations where commercial electronic rights are requested, it may be helpful to call the grantor and to thoroughly explain the request to the copyright holder. Further explanation may ensure that the request is given appropriate consideration.

When rights are granted, and permission contracts are returned, always store them in a safe and accessible place. Some trade publications can have an extremely long lifespan, so it is important to always retain these documents in case any questions arise about a particular use.

SEEKING PERMISSION IN HIGHER EDUCATION PUBLISHING

The process for acquiring rights for a college or higher education product is similar in many ways to acquiring rights for any other publishing product. The copyright holder must be sought and contacted to request permission, and a fee may be requested for use of the material. As in acquiring any type of right, basic copyright principles must be adhered to in determining whether or not permission is needed. *Note:* Permission must also be acquired to use material in photocopied course packs or handouts to be used in the higher education market.

However, changes in technology, as well as changes in the way higher education products are marketed, have added some unique elements to the process. Traditionally, the college product consisted of a textbook(as well as its various accompaniments, such as the instructor's manual, student study guide, a testbank, and transparency masters) or other printed work presented in a straightforward, academic style. The information age and new technologies have now dramatically altered the education market, and publishers often offer software, CD-ROMs, and videos, as well as material delivered over the Internet and other online services. Publishers are discovering new ways to accommodate market demands for the most up-to-date information and individualized teaching tools by offering custom published and on-demand products. This plethora of products presents a variety of challenges in acquiring permissions.

When writing a textbook, it is often the author's contractual obligation to secure all necessary permissions. However, production schedules are usually tight, and authors can be more focused on fine-tuning their manuscript than on sending out permission request letters. Therefore, it is helpful to have a permissions editor available to ensure that all proper legal procedures are followed. The starting point for this process is a review of the manuscript, and it is essential that the reviewer (or a member of the reviewing team) has a solid foundation in copyright law, especially in the area of implementing the company's fair use policies.

This is most important when reviewing manuscripts by novice authors, who may tend to interpret fair use too liberally. It helps to have a set of permissions guidelines to send to authors just after they have signed their contract. The use of certain amounts of material without permission, which may have been acceptable in an academic paper, will often not be acceptable when used in a commercially available product.

The permissions editor should be involved in product planning meetings from the beginning so that there is an accurate account of what rights are required for each project. Including a rights and permissions person at the planning meetings encourages editors and marketing representatives to detail all the forms a product might undertake throughout its lifespan; thus, rights for these uses can be cleared up front. Obtaining these clearances can save time and money on a project in the long run. To request rights, the permissions editor must know if any supplements are planned, if the work will be marketed as one complete text or if a split version will be available, if there will be any software or other electronic versions of the work, as well as the territory and language rights required. Posing these questions during the planning stage will help avoid any future need to clear rights for a use that was not initially considered.

Once the manuscript has been reviewed, and the material requiring permission has been identified, request letters must be prepared. The letter is extremely important because it must ask the recipient for all rights to the material necessary to fulfill the marketing plans for the product. Any territory and language rights needed should also be included. It is customary for these request letters to seek the right to use the material in all current and future editions and versions of the work, in all forms and media, as well as in any supplementary materials. Also, to avoid any potential confusion or problems, the permission request letter should ask for the right to grant limited permissions to third parties who might want to reuse the material as it appears in the work for which permission is being requested (e.g., to nonprofit institutions providing works for print- or hearing-disabled students). Occasionally, all of these rights may be granted. More often, however, rights will be granted for a one-time use in one edition of the work, especially if the work is requested from another publisher. If your project absolutely needs more than this, a person-to-person negotiation is called for. Generally, the rights needed are available, but the fee may increase accordingly. At this point, the permissions editor must decide (in consultation with the author or editor) the value of the particular material to the project.

A record should be kept of all permissions letters sent to the copyright holders. It is helpful to set up a log or other recordkeeping system that will note the date the original letter was sent, the name and address of the rights holder, the response, the fee (which is usually payable upon publication), and whether or not a *complimentary copy* is required. The log can also be used to note if only partial rights were obtained and if another rights holder needs to be contacted (if, for example, the original contact only holds North American rights, and world rights are needed). It is also helpful to record the required *credit lines* as responses are received. This makes it easier for the production staff to set up the acknowledgments page(s). This kind of complete, accurate record will prove invaluable when the work is published, and checks and "comp copies" must be sent to those who granted permission. It will also save a great deal of time when clearing rights for future editions.

The procedures described above apply mostly to standard types of higher education products. *Custom published* products present an altogether different scenario. When seeking permission, the treatment of "one edition" must be addressed, since it is impossible to limit a custom published product to one edition. The nature of custom publishing is to allow the use of a piece of material, anywhere from a single use to multiple uses, as the customer chooses. The permission request should explain this and request a fixed period of time, or term, in which to use the material. A custom publishing program usually provides a mechanism for recording the number of times a specific piece of material is used, so it is possible to establish a fee structure on a per-use basis. Be specific in your request letter by describing what use-tracking mechanism is available, how long the material will be made available to the user and how the material will become part of the custom publishing process. For instance, if the material is to be scanned into a system, your request must articulate that portion of the process.

Electronic products, including both online and stand alone, on the surface should not be problematic. The elements in the request are often the same as a regular text: one edition, a specific number of copies made, distribution in a certain territory (although problematic online), the ability to include an appropriate credit line, and so on. Difficulties arise when the copyright holder of the material becomes concerned about what kind of controls will be instituted to protect its material from being manipulated, scanned, copied electronically, or distributed on a wider network by third parties. These concerns are vexing and sometimes impossible to address completely. It is in these situations that the parties are reliant on the copyright law to provide adequate protection to all electronically delivered material. In general, structure the permissions agreement to provide as much protection as can be reasonably expected and trust in compliance with the copyright law for the rest.

Always remember that signed letters or contracts granting rights to use material are legal documents and should be treated accordingly. Originals or photocopies should be filed so that they are accessible, and they should be retained for the full life of the work. When the work goes out of print, and if rights are returned to the author, check your company policy to see if the permissions file can be sent along with other assignment documents. If the rights are not returned, the permissions file can be stored with other documents that are not used often but need to be kept. There is always a chance of an issue surfacing that will require a check of the original permissions agreement, and the ability to easily locate the document will be valued in terms of time and effort.

SEEKING PERMISSION IN SCHOOL PUBLISHING

There are many issues specific to the acquisition and licensing of rights to use previously published material in textbooks and other educational materials produced for elementary and secondary school markets. This market is commonly called "el-hi."

One of the key distinctions in el-hi publishing is that roughly half of the 50 states make purchasing decisions based on approval by state adoption boards. In such states, there are rigorous requirements for submission and approval of materials that affect nearly every aspect of the publishing process, from scheduling the publication to manufacturing to content. In such adoption states, only educational publications that are approved or "listed" by the adoption boards may be purchased with state monies. Because two of the largest textbook markets (Texas and California) purchase educational books and materials based on state adoption decisions, the implications for educational publishing in meeting the various state requirements are significant.

Implications of textbook purchasing through the state adoption process permeate the acquisition of rights in the following ways:

1. Ensuring that the terms governing the use of previously published material in programs are consistent with the terms of adoption con-

tracts. For example, if a permissions agreement allows for the use of literature or an illustration for five years, but the typical adoption contract for the textbook in which the selection will appear is 10 years or longer, then longer permission licenses should be negotiated. Another example is the requirement that textbooks comply with manufacturing standards and specifications defined by the National Association of State Textbook Administrators (NASTA specs). Occasionally, producing a previously published work in a format suitable for inclusion in a textbook program requires subtle changes that must be negotiated in a permissions or rights agreement.

2. Standards imposed by individual state adoption boards may require that textbook publishers make alterations in previously published text or art that must first be negotiated with the original publisher. Common examples of problematic references or graphics include:

- references to certain political activities;
- alcohol, drugs (including harmless references that are in keeping with the time and place setting of certain fiction);
- references to sexual activity, pregnancy without marriage, bodily functions or phases;
- ethnic or racial slurs even in context;
- references to trade names or games however innocuous or contextually appropriate;
- references in text or illustrations to smoking;
- references in text or illustrations to nudity (this can even be a problem with animals on occasion or in picture books of babies);
- grammar or differences in style or size type faces.

3. Ensuring that the rights acquired for previously published materials allow for the sublicensing of textbooks in which such material appears, and in formats that are accessible for disabled students as described in adoption contracts. Until recently, it was standard procedure to acquire, to the fullest extent possible, the rights to sublicense Braille, large print, and recorded readings of all content in a textbook. However, recent state legislation has broadened both the scope of the formats that must be available, including electronic media, as well as the population served, requiring harmonizing of contractual arrangements in the trade and school publishing industries. Also, new federal legislation has changed copyright owners' claims with regard to the rights of nonprofit organizations and governmental agencies to reproduce and distribute previously published works exclusively for use by blind or other persons with disabilities (*17 U.S.C.– Section 121*).

In terms of general acquisition of rights even in "open territory" (i.e., non-adoption states), the educational market requires an understanding of specific issues. Textbook publishing frequently requires alterations to works as originally published. Examples include:

1. Consolidation of a 32-page picture book into a few pages means that less art will be used ("stacking of text"). The potential problems are as follows:

- losing desirable rhythm/flow of text and pictures;
- losing visual clues that help with decoding and comprehension;
- losing "spaciousness" or other advantages bestowed on a work in its original design;
- changing the "picture book" to an illustrated story;
- book shape and size (horizontal = landscapes, action, and cumulative stories. Square-circular motions = lots happening at same time. Upright rectangle = tall buildings, heights);
- framing/border treatments affect the composition or scale of the art.

However, if a textbook publisher makes changes in a story for an anthology, the original trade publisher can seek approval for the layout and submit it for further approval by the author/illustrator.

2. Potential problems with excerpting full-length juvenile novels or chapter books:

- generally deprecation, giving children diluted tastes of the original;
- using only key excerpts without the context in which theme, plot, and characters are developed;
- making editorial changes (deleting references to story points not relevant to the excerpt);
- textbook editors choose and present excerpts in such a way as to invite readers to read the entire book. Frequently, a cover of the book and bibliographic information accompany the excerpts.

In negotiating rights and permissions for previously published literature, it is important to consider whether and what types of changes are necessary, and to ensure that the negotiations and contracts encompass terms for any such changes. Even acquiring straight reprint licenses for school editions of trade books can necessitate special contractual provisions allowing for certain alterations to meet either NASTA specifications (imprint on cover, addition of folios, weight of paper or cover stock) or school marketing requirements (design elements to integrate or identify titles into overall program or curriculum framework).

In acquiring rights, it is in the best interest of both contracting parties for the acquiring publisher to plan ahead for all anticipated ancillary uses of the material. For example, in nearly all cases, rights to use literature in a student edition also require the right to use the literature in accompanying teacher editions. Other rights that may be required include the use of the text on audiotape, excerpts in teaching or assessment materials including computer software, and the use of selections in languages other than English. Planning ahead for all such uses will streamline the negotiation in the long run and will enable the publisher to determine what rights may simply be unavailable before a commitment to use the selection is in place.

SEEKING PERMISSION FOR COURSE PACKS

As noted earlier, it is also necessary to acquire permission to use copyrighted material in the classroom, such as in course packs, photocopied handouts, web pages, other online or electronic forms, or distance learning transmission. While it is possible that some specific and very limited uses may fall under the fair use exception of the copyright law, most do not, including the systematic creation of course packs. The process for obtaining permission for uses such as these is generally the same as would be used in obtaining permission to use material in a new publication. However, when making your request, the following information should be submitted to the rights holder in addition to information about the material you wish to use:

- the school, course, professor, and semester in which the material will be used;
- the number of copies to be made of the material, if applicable;
- the format in which the material will be used (photocopied, distance learning transmission, appearing on web page); and
- the specifics about those who will have access to the material, if applicable (online or distance learning transmissions, for example).

The license received will usually limit the use of the material to a single semester and a specific use.

COPYRIGHT CLEARANCE CENTER

Registering titles with the Copyright Clearance Center (CCC) at www.copyright.com strengthens your intellectual property protection and can generate additional royalties for your titles and your authors. CCC, a not-for-profit organization formed in 1978 by publishers, authors, and users of copyrighted information, provides a central clearinghouse through which copyright owners and users of copyrighted material exchange permissions and royalties. CCC's licensing services give publishers a practical, cost-effective means to increase revenue by putting under license many copyrighted materials, in both print and digital formats, that would otherwise go unlicensed.

The importance of CCC to publishers was affirmed in the *American Geophysical Union, et al. vs. Texaco* decision, in which the courts applauded the publishing industry for its foresight in establishing CCC, thus negating the administrative burden argument as an infringement defense for users of copyrighted materials.

CCC represents any or all of a publisher's works and can manage rights information at a very detailed level, assisting publishers in meeting their royalty obligations to their authors and other creators. It is advisable to make sure your publishing organization's standard contract with authors makes clear that the materials can be registered with CCC to secure additional protection and royalty income.

CCC can be a useful supplement to your own permission activities. Acting as an agent under individual contracts with publishers and authors, CCC offers licensing services for secondary rights in a variety of specific markets. These licensing services support authorized reproduction for users seeking to use a broad range of copyrighted materials in print or digital formats. In turn, publishers and their authors receive royalty revenues (generally based on fees set by the copyright owners) and detailed usage data.

CCC's web site, http://www.copyright.com, clears rights online for thousands of titles for which publishers have pre-authorized permissions. Customers may search the CCC database of titles and secure permissions instantly. CCC then collects payments and issues royalties to publishers. CCC provides the following copyright licensing services:

- *Annual Authorizations Service* – When you register with this repertory service, CCC grants photocopy permissions for in-house use and collects royalties on your behalf from thousands of corporations, subsidiaries, and law firms.

- *Digital Repertory Service* – If you are already a participant in CCC's Annual Authorizations Service, you can serve the growing market for digital content. This service collects royalties from users who distribute your copyrighted materials on internal electronic networks, such as corporate intranets.

- *Republication Licensing Service* – Register your works with this fully automated, online service and you gain access to a new royalty opportunity for the republication of your works in print or digital formats. Publishers set their own royalty fees while users can request permissions and even pay royalty fees over the Web.

- *Transactional Reporting Service* – Register your publications and CCC grants photocopy permissions and collects royalty fees (set by you) on your behalf for distribution of your copyrighted materials. Because you pre-authorize permissions, users such as academic libraries, document suppliers, companies, and individuals get instant photocopy authorizations.

- *Academic Permissions Service* – Register your works free of charge and CCC provides universities and bookstores with a quick, convenient, one-stop shop for clearing permissions to use your titles in academic coursepacks and classroom handouts.

- *Electronic Course Content Service* – Register your works for this service and CCC grants permissions and collects royalty fees on your behalf for use of your copyrighted works in distance learning, electronic reserves, and electronic coursepacks.

- *Foreign Authorizations Service* – With this service you can extend your royalty opportunities beyond the U.S. by authorizing CCC to grant photocopy permission and collect royalties on your behalf for use of your works in other countries.

- *International Photocopy License* – When you register with this repertory service, CCC grants permissions and collects royalties on your behalf for U.S. organizations' subsidiaries and affiliates in other countries to photocopy copyrighted works for in-house use.

- *Mira — Media Image Resource Alliance —* This online stock image service at mira.com lets rightsholders license copyrighted photos, cartoons, and illustrations over the Web. Copyright holders set their own royalty fees and usage restrictions.

- *Federal Government Photocopy Licensing Service —* CCC grants photocopy permissions to government agencies for in-house use of your registered works and collects royalties on your behalf.

Publishers, authors, and other creators can register their copyrighted materials free of charge for all of the above services.

GRANTING PERMISSION

There are four basic steps to processing permission requests for the permission grantor: determining that your publishing house owns the material for which permission is requested; obtaining all the information you need to respond to the request; issuing the license or other response in accordance with your company policy; and processing the fees and/or other materials required by your license, if any.

Determining What Rights Are Owned in the Material Requested

The first step in processing a permission request is to determine whether you control the necessary rights to grant the requested license. There are two aspects to making this determination. First, the publishing agreement for the book must be checked to determine that you control the specific rights requested (e.g., selection or anthology rights, photocopying rights, electronic rights) in the territory requested. You will also need to verify that the material is still under copyright and that rights to the work have not been sold or reverted to the author. If necessary, a letter should be sent to the requestor referring them to the current rights holder or indicating that the material is in the public domain.

Next, the specific material being requested should be checked to make sure that it is original in the book and not used by permission of some other source. To determine whether or not you own the requested material and can therefore grant permission for it, check a physical copy of the book. Many anthologies and readers are published containing material that belongs to someone else. Also, there are often photos, illustrations, and tabular data that come from other sources, for which you cannot grant permission. The original source of the material will be noted in an acknowledgment, either on the first page of the article or in the acknowledgments section, which may begin on the copyright page and may be continued at the back of the book. In the case of charts, graphs, maps, photos, and illustrations, the credit is usually given below or beside the item. You may get requests for articles, essays, stories, etc., that you do not own, in which case the requestor should be referred to the original source of the material.

Obtaining the Information About the Request

Each publishing house will have its own guidelines regarding what and how much information will be required from the requestor before permission will be granted; however, the information outlined on page 32 in the Permission Seeking section herein is a good guideline to the information your company will probably want. At a minimum, you will need specific information identifying the material for which permission is requested and a description of how the material will be used. If required or pertinent information is missing from the request, the grantor must call or write to the requestor to obtain that information.

Issuing the Grant/Denial

Once you have determined that your company owns the requested material and you have all the information needed to decide on a response, the request should be evaluated to decide whether or not to grant permission and what fee, if any, to charge, in accordance with company policies on granting permission.

Although the conditions under which a permission request may be granted will vary from one kind of reuse to another, the requirements should generally indicate a deliberate and balanced approach and should be applied consistently to each requestor. A detailed list of types of reuse, and the attending permission requirements should be available to the permissions staff. The list of requirements should have the approval of senior management. Requirements should be appropriate to the type of reuse requested. For example, it would be suitable for a granting publisher to require the same level of credit to appear with a reprinted chart, photograph, or short excerpt.

Granting publishers may wish to give special consideration to authors who are seeking permission, perhaps in terms of giving the authors some powers of approval in conjunction with the publisher's permission grants. For example, if an author wants to reuse his/her own previously published article in a new book with a new publisher, the granting publisher may waive any fee requirements associated with this kind of permission. (In waiving any requirements, the granting publisher should always make it clear that specific requirements are in fact being waived to specify its reasons for doing so.) Another example: if a third party requests permission to revise and republish an author's article, the granting publisher may issue a conditional permission, requiring the requestor to also obtain the author's approval before considering the permission final.

Publishers must be aware of how the "work-for-hire" aspects of copyright may affect their permissions policies. For example, if an author is writing about work he/she has performed for his/her employer, the employer may in fact be considered the copyright "author" of the written work, and therefore may be the only one authorized to transfer copyright to the publisher. If this is the case, and assuming that copyright has since been transferred to the publisher, the publisher may then wish to give special consideration to these employers, in terms of giving the employers some powers of approval in conjunction with certain of the publisher's permission grants.

Processing Fees and Other Follow Up

The last part of the permission granting process is to follow up on any licenses that have been issued. This includes processing payments made, reviewing complimentary copies of books to determine that they comply with the terms of a license (especially regarding acknowledgments); and sending out dunning letters and/or canceling licenses that have not been complied with in terms of payment of fees or other requirements.

Permission Granting Issues Specific to Trade Publishing

Granting permission on trade titles involves careful consideration of each request. Many authors and illustrators are concerned with how and where their material is used. It is important to become familiar with these concerns. Some authors do not approve of their work being condensed or excerpted, and other authors may not approve of the particular organization requesting permission and the intended use. The relationship between the author and the publishing company is important, and it is the publisher's responsibility to ensure that the work is not used in a way that embarrasses or upsets the author. Illustrators are especially concerned with the reproduction quality of their artwork. Pay special attention to the artist's concerns when granting permission to use illustrations.

Because authors of trade books frequently retain control of various subsidiary rights to their works, the publisher must review the contract to ensure that the rights requested are controlled by the publisher before granting any request for use of a trade product. *Selection or anthology rights* must be held, as well as any specific right requested. For instance, if the request is to use three pages of a text on a CD-ROM that will be sold both in the United States and abroad, the publisher must control selection rights, as well as electronic rights, throughout the world. If the publisher does not control the necessary rights, the request should be forwarded to the author or the author's agent.

Requests to use material in an electronic format present the possibility for manipulation of the work and should be evaluated closely. Material incorporated in CD-ROMs or software is vulnerable to alteration by users, and multiple users if the software is installed on a network. Not only does this enable slight manipulations of the work, but derivative works can also be created using pieces of text, illustrations, or photographs to create a new work. If the author or publisher is concerned about manipulation of a work, it is best to include strict delineations of allowable uses when granting rights to use material in digital formats.

The valuation of material in trade publications can vary tremendously. Because trade publications incorporate fiction and non-fiction, illustrations, photographs, poetry, letters, and a whole array of both creative and informative literature, it is difficult to establish a uniform procedure for granting rights. A request to use two lines of poetry, for instance, could be considered quite differently from a request to use a chapter from a work explaining the best way to plant a garden. After establishing that rights to the requested material are indeed held by the publisher, a decision on whether or not to grant the request should be made based on the perceived value of the work.

Permission Granting Issues Specific to School Publications

In contrast to licensing rights and permissions for other types of publications, there is considerable overlap involving customer service and public relations concerns when responding to inquiries for use of el-hi publications. The inquiries commonly fall into three categories.

1. Use of el-hi material in other publications. This is the least frequent use, and generally the approach is as follows. Determine what specific material will be used and the extent of rights owned by your publishing house. Educational publications are often comprised largely of material owned by others, and therefore the typical response to such requests is to refer the query to the correct rights holder. If in fact you confirm that your own publishing house controls the necessary rights, then the decision to grant permission will hinge on the nature of the material requested and the proposed use in order to determine whether rights should be granted, and, if so, under what terms. The analysis is similar to that undertaken in granting rights and permissions in general.

2. Use of el-hi material for reproduction (photocopy or otherwise) by customers. This is the most frequent type of inquiry fielded by rights and permissions personnel in el-hi divisions. Generally, responses to such inquiries require close communication with the regional sales offices or field representatives in order to assess customer needs and balance them with both the financial and publishing objectives of the company, and the extent of copyright ownership of the materials in question. In a climate of increasingly tight budgets, with little allowance for the purchase of "consumable" educational materials, and where high-speed economical photocopying/electrocopying and document delivery is increasingly commonplace, these requests are often a means of sidestepping the purchase of materials.

3. Adaption and/or reproduction of educational materials in special formats for the disabled. In a typical year, educational divisions process hundreds of inquiries regarding special formats for the disabled. In 1996, the U.S. publishing industry and organizations representing the blind worked together to develop a workable amendment that uses the strength and flexibility of the copyright law to meet the needs of blind readers. As a result of this cooperative effort, legislation was signed into law that will give blind readers ready access to newly published books and other reading materials. A special exemption to the Copyright Act (creating a new Section 121), allows previously published non-dramatic literary works to be reproduced and distributed in specialized formats for the blind without the need to obtain permission from the copyright holder. This change was signed into law in 1996 as part of a funding bill for the Legislative Branch (including the Library of Congress).

Overall, the acquisition of rights and permissions for educational publications produced for the el-hi market requires equal sensitivity to copyright issues, evaluation of market demands weighed against author or publisher proprietary concerns, and an effort to come up with policies that address both the public need for information, and the need for compensation to the party who created and added value to the material.

Permission Granting Issues Specific to College Text Publishing

As noted earlier, permission is needed to use copyrighted material in course packs in the classroom. All publishers experience a substantial increase in the volume of permission requests received at the start of each college semester, as schools prepare course packs for their students; permission request volume may double or even triple at such times. However, college text publishers face an even greater seasonal increase because they also receive several permission requests that are not for coursepack photocopying. Some of these requests include:

- Permission to photocopy portions of books that have been ordered by the school but are not delivered by the publisher before the course starts. The publisher will generally allow the school to make copies of the portions of the text that will be covered in the class prior to the book's arrival, with the understanding that the students will then purchase the books.

- Permission to create overheads from material in books for use in the classroom.

- Permission to film and/or broadcast material used in a course, generally for distance learning. The material used can be books or journals, text excerpts, videos, overheads, or any other "ancillaries." Courses can be filmed and broadcast on closed-circuit television, local public access or cable channels, or taped and hand-distributed to students.

- Permission to copy or otherwise use nonprint ancillary materials, including videotapes, audiotapes, and software.

- Site licenses for installing software on computer networks or on multiple hard drives.

- Permission to create PowerPoint™ presentations or other digital classroom aids.

- Permission to use material in electronic reserve systems or other closed campus computer networks.

- Permission to post material on course web sites.

For public relations reasons, since these requestors are also the publishers' customers, publishers generally attempt to respond to such requests as quickly and as liberally as possible.

Chapter 4
SUBSIDIARY RIGHTS

Permission licensing is just one example of ancillary or subsidiary rights that may be included in the author's grant of rights to the publisher. Whereas permission licenses are usually granted in response to a request, (for portions of the book), subsidiary rights are considered a proactive sales area.

Much selling takes place when the book is in the manuscript stage. Except for serial sales, most arrangements are for the entire book. The contracts are most often exclusive grants entailing an advance against royalties, as opposed to the non-exclusive, flat-fee structures associated with most permission grants.

The following is a brief overview of subsidiary rights and should by no means be considered an exhaustive treatment of the matter. For further and more detailed information, see Lynette Owen's *Selling Rights* and *The Handbook of International Rights*, developed and written by the members of the AAP International Division Rights and Co-Publishing Committee (see the Bibliography).

WHAT ARE SUBSIDIARY RIGHTS?

The best way to consider subsidiary rights is as all the rights not covered by the primary publishing rights (also referred to as *volume rights*). The primary publishing right is usually defined as the right to exclusively, and for the first time, publish and distribute a book in different volume forms (such as paperback or hardcover), and in an agreed-upon territory. When negotiating for volume rights, it pays to get an exact definition of terms, because opinions differ considerably on this seemingly simple issue. Subsidiary rights may be best defined as those rights that are sublicensed to third parties.

Most subsidiary rights are sold in the form of a license, the exact terms of which are negotiated between the publisher (Licensor) and the

Licensee. The Licensee can be another publisher (in most translation, paperback, or co-publication deals), a movie or video producer (when film, movie, or video rights are licensed), a book club, a journal (in the case of first and second serial rights), or a merchandiser (in the case of merchandizing rights).

The most commonly licensed subsidiary rights are:

- Translation rights
- Co-publication and co-edition rights
- Paperback and reprint rights
- Serial rights (divided into first, second, and one-shot periodical rights)
- Digest and condensation rights
- Anthology and quotation rights (permissions)
- Electronic publishing rights
- Dramatization and documentary rights (including theatrical rights, radio rights, movie rights, and television rights)
- Videotape and audio cassettee rights
- Merchandizing rights
- Visually handicapped rights
- Large print rights

This list is by no means exhaustive. The potential list of rights is infinite, and new rights will undoubtedly be developed and licensed in the future. A case in point is the hotly debated area of electronic rights, which are now beginning to be exploited.

In this section, more emphasis will be given to those rights sold most frequently, such as book club, paperback, or co-publication rights. In addition, there is also a brief outline and definition of each of the other subsidiary rights. The reader should bear in mind that many variations are possible in each case, and that each different license depends on a variety of different circumstances, such as publisher involvement (large trade house, textbook publisher, el-hi publisher, fiction publisher, university press, small press, etc.), as well as the book and the particular author in question. It is obvious that selling first serial rights to a Gloria Steinem book to *Ms.* magazine will be a very different enterprise than selling first serial rights to a scientific book to *Nature* magazine.

One important tip when selling subsidiary rights is the crucial importance of an intimate knowledge of the original contract between author and publishing house, since all future licensing activities will be based on this document. Anyone selling rights has to spend a considerable amount of time rigorously examining the original grant of rights and ensuring that there will be no conflicts of interest down the road. The same is true for old licenses, all of which have to be carefully checked to make sure that any new license will not conflict with an existing "exclusive" license. Selling rights begins and ends with impeccable record keeping, and whenever there is doubt, make no assumptions, check the documents. It always pays to do extensive legwork, which may include first clarifying certain issues with an author, an agent, or another publisher. Once a license is signed, it may turn out to be extremely difficult to cancel such a license.

BOOK CLUB RIGHTS

In a typical book club license, a publisher licenses to a book club the right to print and distribute a particular book to that club's membership. For a publisher, this can mean welcome and added revenue, both in terms of the advance as well as reducing the printing costs of a book, if the club chooses to purchase copies of the book from the publisher rather than reprinting it. Also, a book club can often introduce a book to a very specific audience, which the publisher may otherwise not be able to reach.

Book club members can usually buy a book at a reduced price, but one of the chief advantages of being a book club member is the club's important referee, review, and gatekeeping function.

Some of the major players in the U.S. are: the Book-of-the-Month club (and such well-known clubs as the History Book Club and the Quality Paperback Book Club), The Literary Guild, and the Newbridge Communication Book Clubs (including the Library of Science Book Club, the Natural Science Book Club, the Archeology Book Club, Readers Subscription, Garden Book Club, and others). There are many small specialty book clubs, such as the Catholic Book Club, the Jewish Book Club, or the Chemical Engineering Book Club. For a more detailed list, consult the book club section in the current *Literary Market Place*.

Depending on the deal and on the club, book club rights are licensed either as "exclusive" (meaning you cannot license to another book club) or as "nonexclusive" (you can license to others). Depending on the original rights granted to the publishers, and depending on where the book club plans to sell the book, book club rights may be licensed worldwide or they may be restricted to a certain territory. Sometimes, the club will manufacture their own special club edition (with the publisher's film). At other times, the club will simply run-on with the publisher's print run, an arrangement that is usually cost effective for both parties. A license is usually restricted to a certain number of years, and the contract determines whether or not the club can sell the book prior to publication. Book club rights are usually sold for an advance against royalties of copies sold, but all sorts of other creative solutions are possible, such as selling at a "royalty inclusive unit price" when small quantities are involved.

TRANSLATION RIGHTS

In a typical translation license, a publisher licenses to another publisher the right to translate a book into another language and to publish it within an agreed-upon territory. Translation licenses usually have a life of five to seven years and are almost always exclusive. The license usually stipulates that publication of the foreign language edition has to occur within a specified period of time (usually 18–24 months), and, depending on the country and the publisher, a license may also include certain subsidiary rights in that particular language, such as reprint or book club rights. Sometimes such subsidiary rights are specifically excluded and will only be granted after an additional contract has been signed.

The overall goal of signing a translation contract is to increase a book's impact by making it available in another language and exposing it to another market. Some of the most important questions to ask are: Will the foreign publisher publish a successful foreign language edition of my book? Will the translation be good? Will they be able to sell and market the book well in their respective territory?

Especially in recent years, it has become obvious that selling multiple translation rights can generate a significant source of income for a publisher. This is why translation rights are often retained by authors and handled through their agents on a commission basis.

Translation rights are sold directly from publisher to publisher, or exclusively through a subagent. Publishers often rely on a combination of approaches in order to preserve flexibility. Some publishers have subagents represent their whole list; others let subagents only handle books on a title-by-title basis. Some publishers work exclusively with one agency in one country, but with several agents in another country. The agent usually receives a commission of the sale and the royalties, and is generally responsible for collecting and administering moneys and royalties. If the agent is reliable, this obviously can be an invaluable service, as it saves the publisher many bureaucratic headaches. At other times, an agent is superfluous, and can even make transactions between two publishers more cumbersome.

There are two other elements in the translation rights selling process that are becoming more and more important: scouts and agencies. A literary scout is usually employed by one or several foreign publishing houses, usually in different countries (because of the competition factor). It is the scout's job to look for appropriate titles for their publishers and occasionally to get involved in the actual rights negotiations. It is therefore extremely important to be knowledgeable about which scouts work for which companies, and to stay in constant touch with the most important scouts. The scouts are an excellent tool for approaching foreign publishers outside the normal channels of selling rights.

Agencies that represent foreign or U.K. publishers operate in a way similar to scouts, but on a larger scale. Some scouts operate out of their homes and only work for one or two publishing houses. Depending on the scout/publisher relationship, the scout or agency may, in some cases, also assume selling activities, that is, trying to sell the foreign publisher's books in the United States.

For a more detailed account of the translation business, see Chapter 16 of Owen's *Selling Rights*, which provides more details about translation rights, and Chapter 8 on book fairs and sales trips (see Appendix A, p.95). The latter chapter is also recommended, in light of the fact that the Frankfurt Book Fair is the single most important event for selling translation rights. Being well prepared for the Frankfurt Fair is crucial to any successful foreign rights operation. Book Expo America, a convention and trade exhibition, is also an important event for the publishing industry.

CO-PUBLICATIONS

Unless the author has already entered into a separate contract with another English language publisher, it is up to the original publisher to decide if it is advantageous to sell English language rights in other key markets. This typically includes the sale of rights to a U.K. publisher in Great Britain, Australia, Canada, or South Africa. These arrangements help to distribute the book widely, especially if the U.K. publisher has a better market presence in the designated territories than the U.S. partner. After careful negotiations to define the territories, each party has to restrict its marketing efforts to its designated territory. The actual rights sale usually consists of an advance against royalties and a grant of certain specific subsidiary rights in each territory.

Depending on the arrangement and on the publisher, a co-publication might also involve coordinating various production aspects of a book. The arrangement then becomes much more than a simple rights deal, especially when complex production matters need to be coordinated, and careful negotiations regarding the unit price, shipping costs, and other expenses are required. Such a joint venture can be especially profitable when publishing an expensive and lavishly illustrated art or photo book, because the co-publication reduces the costs for both parties. On the other hand, the British publisher may decide to discontinue the co-edition relationship with the U.S. publisher and instead buy the film and produce its own copies.

For more details, the AAP's *Handbook of International Rights* provides an overview and discusses various sample agreements. Lynette Owen's *Selling Rights* also has an excellent chapter, "Same Language Territorial Rights" (Chapter 9), that should be consulted on the particulars of selling co-publication rights.

PAPERBACK AND REPRINT RIGHTS

Licensing paperback rights usually implies the sale of rights by a hardcover publisher to a paperback publisher. Reprint rights are the rights to publish a work that might already be out of print or to license a publisher in a developing country to locally produce an inexpensive version of the work.

While publishers generally sell paperback rights proactively, they usually sell reprint rights only when there is an expressed interest. Paperback rights and reprint rights are usually sold for an advance against a royalty, and for a limited period of time, sometimes until the book goes out of print. Other arrangements are possible, such as a one-time fee for a small reprint by another publisher, or an agreement for a fee for a second printing should this need arise. If the reprinting party uses the publisher's edition for offsetting their edition, an offset fee is sometimes negotiated.

FIRST AND SECOND SERIAL RIGHTS AND ONE-SHOT PERIODICAL RIGHTS

Serial rights are rights for extracts, or a series of extracts sold to a magazine or journal, which either prints them before publication (first serial rights) or after the work is published (second serial rights). One-shot periodical rights allow the printing of the whole text of a work in one journal or magazine issue. Fees for all of these rights vary greatly according to the popularity of the piece that is printed, the author, and the journal or magazine that is involved. For some books, serial rights are sold at a high price and auctioned off among various parties. For others, serial rights are used mostly as a marketing tool to generate additional publicity for the book.

DIGEST AND CONDENSATION RIGHTS

Digest and condensation rights are the right to condense the text of a literary work and publish a shorter version of it in a magazine or a journal. One example of a major purchaser of such rights is Reader's Digest Association, Inc.

ANTHOLOGY AND QUOTATION RIGHTS

Anthology rights are the licensing of material to a publisher to use a portion or portions of a copyrighted work in an anthology (see Chapter 3, "Permission Licenses"). Depending on the length and the importance of the section, some rightsholders may charge a small royalty rate on each copy sold rather than a one-time permission fee.

Quotation rights enable a purchaser to quote portions of copyrighted works. There is continual debate about when one must seek permission from the publisher, and when a quote can be considered fair use.

ELECTRONIC PUBLISHING RIGHTS

This is perhaps one of the most exciting new areas in publishing, but it is still in development, with many disputes. Electronic rights is a topic drawing large crowds at seminars, meetings, and conventions.

Licensing electronic rights takes on several forms. It can mean licensing copyrighted material onto various electronic formats: CD-ROM, software (floppy disk), online database (including the Internet) laser disc, hypertext, videodisc, digital storage, or hand-held devices (these are the principal media). It can also include rights to digitize and store copyrighted material for document delivery, on-site display, and custom publishing/print-on-demand systems. Many of these media issues are the focus of debate on how to disseminate and preserve copyrighted works in an electronic age. However, publishing houses are entering into various types of electronic rights agreements on a more regular basis. For some electronic rights deals, there is something of a common ground for acquiring and granting rights.

Certain houses are granting rights for CD-ROM, floppy disk, laser disc, videodisc, and online databases. When requesting to use material on a CD-ROM, floppy disk, laser disc, or videodisc, the grantor will want to know the following information:

- lifetime printing/sales of the product,
- selling price of the product,
- type of market and territory that you want to sell to,
- running time/length of the product (if applicable)
- other than the material you are requesting, the type of material that will be included in the product,
- whether your product is protected from downloading capability/copying.

Depending on the type of use, the grantor's licensing options include a one-time permission fee or a royalty-based agreement.

When requesting material for online use, the grantor will want to know the following information:

- the length of time you want the material to appear on your online site,
- whether your site requires a secured password,
- how many hits a day/month/year your site gets,
- the other types of material that appear on your site.

The grantor will usually issue a license with a one-time permission fee for online use.

These examples of electronic rights are very general and the rightsholder/granter will vary as to how they will handle each request. Because new media and new forms of communication are constantly changing, it is extremely important to keep up-to-date in this field, to watch trends closely, and to be specific in licensing language regarding uses being authorized and those not authorized.

DRAMATIZATION AND DOCUMENTARY RIGHTS

This too is a vast area, so this section gives an overview of the different kinds of rights and a brief definition of what they entail.

Theatrical rights are the rights permitting performance of a work on stage whether written in theatrical form, or yet to be adapted for theatrical performance, such as a novel or a short story. Compensation for such rights may come in the form of a percentage of the box office receipts, or a predetermined fee based on the number of scheduled performances. Of course, other arrangements are possible.

Radio rights are sold when written material that has been published is broadcast over the radio, for example, by National Public Radio or the BBC. Whereas the BBC has a per-minute payment system, other radio licenses may have to be negotiated individually, depending on the importance of the material, the author, and the length of the material requested.

Movie rights are usually acquired on an option basis, which will give a producer or a studio the option to develop a product over a certain period of time. The option usually runs for a year, but may be extended for an additional price that is negotiated at the outset. While a producer's option is in play, he or she will look into the viability of the product, whether or how the project can be financed, which actors would be suitable, etc. The vast majority of options expire without a film ever being developed. The option fee is usually an advance against the final "pick up" price of the film, a sum that can be difficult to estimate at the beginning of a project. It is therefore advisable to consult with somebody experienced in this area. Again, this is a vast area, with an array of options regarding negotiating rights, and it is hard to generalize in a brief summary all of the complexities and considerations in this area. A publisher with little or no experience should seek advice from experts, for the actual negotiations as well as for the final contract. For an excellent and detailed discussion, see Chapter 21 of Owen's *Selling Rights*.

Television rights are licensed for the purpose of adapting a copyrighted work for use on television. The same caveats apply as those for negotiating movie rights.

VIDEOTAPES AND AUDIOCASSETTES

Video rights are those licensed to a video producer in order to use a book as a source for inclusion in a particular videotape. Only certain books will lend themselves to this kind of approach, and it is likely that videotape rights will be granted to the same entity producing a film, a theater play, or a television production.

A much wider type of book is licensed for audio rights (single voice/ nondramatic recording). An increasing number of publishers now publish audiotapes, and these rights are usually licensed for an advance against a royalty, depending on the number of copies sold.

MERCHANDIZING RIGHTS

Merchandizing rights are the rights to license the use of a character, a figure, a design, or a particular part of one medium into another medium. For example, Beatrix Potter or her estate might sign an agreement to license her figures for such uses as stuffed toys, posters, wallpaper, and other products. Another example is the use of a particular illustration from a book (a bird illustration from a bird guide to Costa Rica, for example) requested by the Costa Rica Tourist Board Advertising Agency to put on T-shirts. This is a field full of surprises and new ideas, so it pays to be flexible in your arrangements. How merchandizing rights are licensed depends on several different factors, such as the nature of the organization, how a particular item is going to be used, who is going to use it, how the product is going to be distributed, how it is going to be sold, the duration or term of the agreement, and so forth. Again, the licensing agreement should be as specific as possible without stifling the Licensee's business in any way.

VISUALLY HANDICAPPED RIGHTS

These rights usually comprise Braille rights and nondramatic recordings for people who cannot read or hold books without assistance. As a result of cooperative effort between the U.S. publishing industry and organizations representing the blind, legislation was signed into law on September 18, 1996, that permits authorized entities to reproduce or to distribute copies of previously published, nondramatic literary works in specialized formats (including Braille, audio, or digital text) exclusively for use by the blind or other persons with disabilities. Authorized entities are nonprofit organizations or governmental agencies whose primary mission is to provide specialized services for the blind.

LARGE PRINT RIGHTS

Large print rights do not usually fall under visually handicapped rights because they are licensed by publishing houses specializing in these editions for an identified commercial market.

DISTANCE EDUCATION

Under the Digital Millennium Copyright Act (see page 6), the U.S. Copyright Office was mandated to conduct a study of the copyright implications of promoting distance education through interactive digital networks. In May 1999, after six months of hearings, meetings, and demonstrations involving a broad range of interested parties, the U.S. Register of Copyrights released the Copyright Office's findings and recommendations resulting from its study. (The complete report and appendices can be found on the Copyright Office website at http:// www.loc.gov/copyright.)

Chapter 5
REVERSION OF RIGHTS

Generally, when an author signs a contract with a publisher, he gives the publisher the right to exploit certain of his rights under the copyright law, e.g., to publish the book in one or more editions or formats. Eventually, a time may come when either the publisher is no longer interested in publishing the work or, less frequently, the author no longer wishes that publisher to publish his work. At that point, the author generally wishes to obtain his rights back from the publisher. Although the terms of some author contracts provide for automatic reversion when certain conditions are met, frequently publishers either must or prefer to execute an assignment document that explicitly states the terms of the reversion (an assignment of rights). These reversion rights should not be confused with statutory copyright termination rights. The latter exist in addition to contractually agreed-upon reversions, and are provisions fixed in the law that give grantors (authors) absolute rights to terminate grants even if contractual language "waives" such rights. See the discussion of these rights in Chapter 1.

AUTOMATIC REVERSION OF RIGHTS

Some author contracts provide for an automatic reversion of rights when the book goes out of print after certain conditions are met. Generally, the author must be notified in writing that the work is officially out of print; the author must then send the publisher a written demand to place the work back in print, and if the publisher does not do so within a specified period (such as six months), rights to the work automatically revert to the author. If the publisher relies on this automatic reversion, it must ensure that the book is in fact out of print in all editions it publishes or published by its licensees before the out-of-print notice is sent, and it must be sure to carefully track when the automatic reversion occurs to make sure that all appropriate parties within the publishing house are informed of the reversion.

VOLUNTARY REVERSION OF RIGHTS

Some author contracts do not provide for automatic reversion of rights to the author. However, there are occasions when a publisher wishes to revert rights via an assignment document rather than relying on automatic reversion, or instances when an author wishes his rights back even though the publisher has not yet declared his work out of print. Generally, a publisher will revert rights pursuant to a request by the author or his successor in interest. Such requests are often prompted by a notice from the publisher that the work has been declared out of print.

When a publisher receives a request for a reversion, it must: (1) verify that the person requesting it is in fact the party to whom rights should revert (either a party to the publishing agreement/author contract or the successor in interest to such a party); (2) verify that the work in question is out of print, and that all interested parties within the publishing house agree to release the rights; and (3) execute an assignment document and contract termination. The entity to whom the rights have reverted should record the assignment with the Copyright Office.

REVERSION PROCEDURES

1. Review the reversion request to see if reversion is possible. Generally, publishers prefer to have a formal written request for reversion. When a reversion request is received by the publishing house's department responsible for processing it, the staff must first determine whether the requestor is entitled to a reversion, and whether the house wishes to release the rights, before proceeding. The following is a general outline of steps that the publisher will likely follow:

- Verify that the publisher still controls rights to the work. The publisher should confirm that rights have not previously reverted to the author or been sold to another publisher. If rights have been transferred, the publisher will want to notify the requestor of the previous reversion or sale, providing relevant documents, if desired.

- Verify that the requestor is a party eligible for reversion. Generally, this is the party from whom the publisher obtained rights under the publishing agreement (author contract), or that party's successor. Note that there may be several authors who are parties to the publishing agreement. In the absence of terms in the publishing agreement or written instructions signed by all authors to the contrary, rights should revert jointly to all parties to the publishing agreement or their successors in interest. This is true even if only one of the authors requests reversion. However, rights should revert only to material contributed by the party under the publishing agreement. For instance, if text and illustrations were prepared by different persons under different publishing agreements, only text rights should be reverted to the text author. Likewise, when a book has multiple editions with different authors, each author should only be assigned rights to those editions to which he/she contributed.

Note that the actual author of the work is not always a party to the publishing agreement, and therefore is not necessarily an appropriate candidate for reversion. Following are some examples of situations when the author is not an appropriate candidate for reversion.

- The author prepared the work as part of his or her employment, and the employer contracted with the publisher to publish the work. In that case, rights should revert only to the employer, at the employer's request, unless the publisher receives written authorization from the employer to revert rights to the author.

- The author assigned his or her rights in the work to a third party such as his/her children or a charitable institution. In that case, rights should revert only to the party to whom the author assigned those rights (the author's successor in interest), and at that party's request, unless the publisher receives written authorization from the successor to revert rights to the author.

- The author is deceased, in which case the publisher should obtain a copy of the death certificate or other evidence of death. Rights should then revert to either the author's estate or to the heirs listed in the author's will (the author's successor(s) in interest). The publisher should obtain a copy of the will if rights are to revert to specific heirs.

2. Obtain approval for the reversion from all relevant departments within the publishing house. Generally, the person processing the reversion should confirm that the book is out of print and that the book's editor/publishing division has no plans to reprint the work and agrees to release rights to the work. In addition, authorization should be obtained from any department within the publishing house that licenses or grants rights, including subsidiary rights and foreign rights.

Note that it is generally advisable to get formal written authorization from all relevant parties agreeing to the reversion.

It is not uncommon for a publishing house to agree to revert general rights but to retain certain rights (for instance, those for which it has active licenses with other publishers). This information should be provided by the licensing department to the person processing the reversion.

3. Prepare the reversion documents. Once it has been determined which rights, if any, may be reverted, and that the requestor is an appropriate party to whom rights may be reverted, an assignment document should be drawn up. It will probably include the following:

- the title, author(s), copyright date, and copyright certificate number of each work for which rights are being assigned;
- the name of each party to whom rights are being assigned;
- the date of the contract under which rights are being assigned;
- a clear recitation of what rights, if any, are being retained by the publisher;
- language that effectively transfers the rights to the assignees;
- the signature of an authorized representative of the publisher.

A contract termination letter should also be executed that formally terminates the author contract in question; this document should contain the same basic information as the assignment of rights, but should also be signed by the author(s). Once the assignment document is executed, it should be recorded with the U.S. Copyright Office. A document cover sheet must also be sent with any documents submitted for recordation to the Copyright Office (the form is provided by the Copyright Office). The Copyright Office will return the recorded document with a certificate of recordation in approximately one year.

Chapter 6
INTERNATIONAL COPYRIGHTS

HOW U.S. WORKS ARE PROTECTED THROUGHOUT THE WORLD

There is no "international copyright" that automatically protects an author's writings throughout the world. Protection against unauthorized use in a particular country depends, basically, on the national laws of that country. Most countries, however, do offer protection to foreign works under certain conditions, and these conditions have been greatly simplified by international copyright treaties and conventions. Countries that maintain copyright relations with the United States are listed on pages 76–84.

The United States belongs to the two seminal, multilateral copyright treaties – the Universal Copyright Convention (UCC) and the Berne Convention for the Protection of Literary and Artistic Works.

The United States was a founding member of the UCC, which came into force in the U.S. on September 16, 1955. Generally, a work by a national or domiciliary of a country that is a member of the UCC, or a work first published in a UCC country, may claim protection under the UCC.

By joining the Berne Convention on March 1, 1989, the United States gained protection for its authors in all member nations of the Berne Union with which the United States formerly had either no copyright relations or only bilateral treaty arrangements. Members of the Berne Union agree to provide certain minimum levels of copyright protection, and to provide the same minimum levels of protection for nationals of other member countries as they provide their own nationals. A work first published in the United States or another Berne Union country (or first published in a non-Berne country, followed by publication within 30 days in a Berne country) is eligible for protection in all Berne member countries. There are no special requirements or prerequisites (formalities) to protection. For information on the legislation implementing the

Berne Convention, request Circular 93 from the U.S. Copyright Office; Circular 38 also provides the names of all countries with whom the U.S. has copyright relations.

An author who seeks protection for his or her work in a particular country should first research the extent of protection of foreign works in that country. If possible, this should be done before the work is first published anywhere because protection may often depend on the facts existing at the time of such first publication.

If the country in which protection is sought is a party to one of the international copyright conventions, the work may generally be protected by complying with the conditions of the convention. Even if the work is not eligible for protection under an international convention, protection under the specific provisions of the country's national laws may still be possible. Some countries, however, offer little or no copyright protection for foreign works, or little or no effective enforcement for the rights that are statutorily protected.

HIGHLIGHTS OF THE BERNE CONVENTION

The Berne Convention provisions can be roughly divided into three general types: (1) specific rights for authors and proprietors that member countries must provide for in national laws, either by legislation or direct application of the convention, depending on the country's legal system; (2) more general rules that also obligate member countries to adopt national laws consistent with the minimum standards; and (3) optional rights whose adoption is left entirely to the discretion of member countries.

Exclusive of administrative provisions, the Berne Convention contains 20 articles. These articles define the subject matter of protection; set out the points that give rise to the obligations to protect these works (basic eligibility); establish the rule of national treatment; enumerate certain minimum rights authors enjoy which must be given effect in national laws; establish specific opportunities to exempt certain uses from the minimum rights guaranteed by the convention; and describe special rights provisions relating to motion pictures and a few other categories of works.

BASIC PRINCIPLES OF THE BERNE CONVENTION

The Berne Convention has undergone major revision five times to upgrade its obligations due to changed conditions and technological developments affecting authors' rights, and with each successive text, has generally improved and extended the rights of authors and copyright proprietors.

The original Berne Convention was adopted to promote the development of copyright laws for the benefit of authors under a rubric of worldwide copyright protection. Its goal was (and is): the removal of reciprocity as a basis for rights in lieu of national treatment, that is, the elimination of discrimination in rights against foreign authors in all countries; the reduction of formal requirements for the recognition and protection of copyright in foreign works; and the promotion of uniform international legislation for the protection of literary and artistic works.

The two cardinal principles that the Convention first established, both of which have continuing vitality today, are the concept of a union and the rule of national treatment. The rule of national treatment provides that authors at a minimum enjoy the same protection for their works in other countries as those countries accord their own authors.

Authors and others often make inquiries with the Copyright Office seeking "international copyright" protection. Adherence to the Berne Convention brought U.S. authors into a system of automatic protection throughout the world (even in the absence of any "international copyright"). International protection (i.e., the protection for U.S. works abroad) still depends largely on the national laws of the country in which protection is sought and whether or not that country belongs to a treaty or bilateral agreement that obligates it to protect foreign works. The World Trade Agreement (WTO) signed in 1994 included important copyright and other intellectual property protection and enforcement obligations as well. These were contained in the WTO side agreement known as the TRIPs agreement.

WIPO COPYRIGHT AND PERFORMANCES & PHONOGRAMS TREATIES

The Diplomatic Conference of the World Intellectual Property Organization (WIPO), which met in Geneva in December 1996, adopted two international treaties designed to encourage the use of international computer networks while establishing a framework for copyright protection in cyberspace. The WIPO Copyright Treaty and the WIPO Performance and Phonograms Treaty, approved by delegates from 160 nations, will strengthen minimum copyright law standards in cyberspace and establish new international norms for the protection of sound recordings (including audio books). The WIPO Treaties have little direct impact on U.S. copyright law, which already fulfills most of the standards set out in the new agreement. However, legislation (see page 6– DMCA) to implement the treaties was passed by Congress in 1998 to bring the U.S. into full compliance with the Treaties. Thirty (30) countries must ratify the Treaties before they are considered effective. At the time of publication, the following countries have ratified the WIPO Copyright Treaty: Argentina, Belarus, Burkina Faso, El Salvador, Hungary, Indonesia, Kyrgyzstan, Panama, Republic of Moldova, Saint Lucia, Slovenia, and the United States of America. For an updated list of countries that have ratified the Treaties: http:// www.wipo.org/eng/ratific/s-copy.htm.

INTERNATIONAL COPYRIGHT RELATIONS OF THE UNITED STATES

The following is a list of formal copyright relations between the United States and other independent nations throughout the world (from U.S. Copyright Office Circular 38). Each entry gives the country name (and alternate name) and a statement of copyright relations. The following code is used:

Berne   Party to the Berne Convention for the Protection of Literary and Artistic Works as of the date given. Appearing within parentheses is the latest Act of the Convention to which the country is a party. The effective date for the United States was March 1, 1989. The latest Act of the Convention to which the United States is a party is the revision done at Paris on July 24, 1971.

Bilateral   Bilateral copyright relations with the United States by virtue of a proclamation or treaty, as of the date given. Where there is more than one proclamation or treaty, only the date of the first one is given.

BAC   Party to the Buenos Aires Convention of 1910, as of the date given. U.S. ratification deposited with the Government of Argentina, May 1, 1911; proclaimed by the President of the United States, July 13, 1914.

None   No copyright relations with the United States.

Phonogram Party to the Convention for the Protection of Producers of Phonograms Against Unauthorized Duplication of Their Phonograms, Geneva, 1971, as of the date given. The effective date for the United States was March 10, 1974.

SAT   Party to the Convention Relating to the Distribution of Programme-Carrying Signals transmitted by Satellite, Brussels, 1974, as of the date given. The effective date for the United States was March 7, 1985.

UCC Geneva Party to the Universal Copyright Convention, Geneva, 1952, as of the date given. The effective date for the United States was September 16, 1955.

UCC Paris Party to the Universal Copyright Convention as revised in Paris, 1971, as of the date given. The effective date for the United States was July 10, 1974.

Unclear   Became independent since 1943. Has not established copyright relations with the United States, but may be honoring obligations incurred under former political status.

WTO   Member of the World Trade Organization, established pursuant to the Marrakesh Agreement of April 5, 1994, to implement the Uruguay Round Agreements. These Agreements affect, among other things, intangible property rights, including copyright and other intellectual property rights. The effective date of United States membership in the WTO is January 1, 1995. A country's membership in the World Trade Organization is effective as of the date indicated.

❖❖❖

RELATIONS AS OF MARCH 3, 2000

Afghanistan
　　None
Albania
　　Berne March 6, 1994 (Paris)
Algeria
　　UCC Geneva August 28, 1973
　　UCC Paris July 10, 1974
　　Berne April 19, 1998 (Paris)
Andorra
　　UCC Geneva Sept. 16, 1955
Angola
　　WTO Nov. 23, 1996
Antigua and Barbuda
　　WTO January 1, 1995
Argentina
　　Bilateral August 23, 1934
　　BAC April 19, 1950
　　UCC Geneva Feb. 13, 1958
　　Berne June 10, 1967 (Brussels)
　　Phonogram June 30, 1973
　　WTO January 1, 1995
　　Berne February 19, 2000 (Paris)
Armenia
　　UCC Geneva May 27, 1973*
　　SAT December 3, 1993
Australia
　　Bilateral March 15, 1918
　　Berne April 14, 1928 (Paris)
　　UCC Geneva May 1, 1969
　　Phonogram June 22, 1974
　　UCC Paris February 28, 1978
　　SAT October 26, 1990
　　WTO January 1, 1995
Austria
　　Bilateral September 20, 1907
　　Berne October 1, 1920
　　UCC Geneva July 2, 1957
　　SAT August 6, 1982
　　UCC Paris August 14, 1982
　　Phonogram August 21, 1982
　　WTO January 1, 1995
Azerbaijan
　　UCC Geneva May 27, 1973*
　　Berne June 4, 1999

Bahamas, The
　　Berne July 10, 1973 (Brussels)
　　UCC Geneva Dec. 27, 1976
　　UCC Paris Dec. 27, 1976
Bahrain
　　WTO January 1, 1995
　　Berne March 2, 1997 (Paris)
Bangladesh
　　UCC Geneva August 5, 1975
　　UCC Paris August 5, 1975
　　WTO January 1, 1995
　　Berne May 4, 1999 (Paris)
Barbados
　　UCC Geneva June 18, 1983
　　UCC Paris June 18, 1983
　　Berne July 30, 1983 (Paris)
　　Phonogram July 29, 1983
　　WTO January 1, 1995
Belarus
　　UCC Geneva May 27, 1973*
　　Berne December 12, 1997 (Paris)
Belau
　　See **Palau**
Belgium
　　Berne Dec. 5, 1887 (Brussels)
　　Bilateral July 1, 1891
　　UCC Geneva August 31, 1960
　　WTO January 1, 1995
　　Berne September 29, 1999 (Paris)
Belize
　　UCC Geneva Dec. 1, 1982
　　WTO January 1, 1995
Benin (formerly Dahomey)
　　Berne January 3, 1961 (Paris)
　　WTO February 22, 1996
Bhutan
　　None
Bolivia
　　BAC May 15, 1914
　　UCC Geneva March 22, 1990
　　UCC Paris March 22, 1990
　　Berne Nov. 4, 1993 (Paris)
　　WTO September 13, 1995

Bosnia and Herzegovina
UCC Geneva May 11, 1966
UCC Paris July 10, 1974
Berne March 6, 1992 (Paris)
SAT March 6, 1992

Botswana
WTO May 31, 1995
Berne April 15, 1998 (Paris)

Brazil
BAC August 31, 1915
Berne February 9, 1992 (Paris)
Bilateral April 2, 1957
UCC Geneva January 13, 1960
Phonogram Nov. 28, 1975
UCC Paris Dec. 11, 1975
WTO January 1, 1995

Brunei Darussalam
WTO January 1, 1995

Bulgaria
Berne December 5, 1921 (Paris)
UCC Geneva July 7, 1975
UCC Paris June 7, 1975
Phonogram September 6, 1995
WTO December 1, 1996

Burkina Faso (formerly Upper Volta)
Berne August 19, 1963 (Paris)
Phonogram January 30, 1988
WTO June 3, 1995

Burma
See **Myanmar, Union of**

Burundi
WTO July 23, 1995

Cambodia
UCC Geneva Sept. 16, 1955

Cameroon
Berne Sept. 21, 1964 (Paris)
UCC Geneva May 1, 1973
UCC Paris July 10, 1974
WTO December 13, 1995

Canada
Bilateral January 1, 1924
Berne Apr. 10, 1928 (Brussels)
UCC Geneva August 10, 1962
WTO January 1, 1995
Berne June 26, 1998 (Paris)

Cape Verde
Berne July 7, 1997 (Paris)

Central African Republic
Berne Sept. 3, 1977 (Paris)
WTO May 31, 1995

Chad
Berne Nov. 25, 1971 (Brussels)
WTO October 19, 1996

Chile
Bilateral May 25, 1896
BAC June 14, 1955
UCC Geneva Sept. 16, 1955
Berne June 5, 1970 (Paris)
Phonogram March 24, 1977
WTO January 1, 1995

China
Bilateral January 13, 1904
Bilateral March 17, 1992
Berne October 15, 1992
UCC Geneva October 30, 1992
UCC Paris October 30, 1992
Phonogram April 30, 1993

Colombia
BAC December 23, 1936
UCC Geneva June 18, 1976
UCC Paris June 18, 1976
Berne March 7, 1988 (Paris)
Phonogram May 16, 1994
WTO April 30, 1995

Comoros
Unclear

Congo
Berne May 8, 1962 (Paris)
WTO March 27, 1997

Costa Rica
Bilateral October 19, 1899
BAC November 30, 1916
UCC Geneva Sept. 16, 1955
Berne June 10, 1978 (Paris)
UCC Paris March 7, 1980
Phonogram June 17, 1982
WTO January 1, 1995

Cote d'Ivoire (Ivory Coast)
Berne January 1, 1962 (Paris)
WTO January 1, 1995

Croatia
UCC Geneva May 11, 1966
UCC Paris July 10, 1974
Berne October 8, 1991 (Paris)
SAT October 8, 1991

Cuba

Bilateral November 17, 1903
UCC Geneva June 18, 1957
WTO April 20, 1995
Berne February 20, 1997 (Paris)

Cyprus

Berne February 24, 1964 (Paris)
UCC Geneva Dec. 19, 1990
UCC Paris December 19, 1990
Phonogram Sept. 30, 1993
WTO July 30, 1995

Czech Republic

UCC Geneva January 6, 1960
UCC Paris April 17, 1980
Berne January 1, 1993 (Paris)
Phonogram January 1, 1993
WTO January 1, 1995

Czechoslovakia

(also see Czech Republic and Slovakia)
Bilateral March 1, 1927

Democratic Republic of Congo

(formerly Zaire)
Berne October 8, 1963 (Paris)
Phonogram November 29, 1977
WTO January 1, 1997

Denmark

Bilateral May 8, 1893
Berne July 1, 1903 (Paris)
UCC Geneva February 9, 1962
Phonogram March 24, 1977
UCC Paris July 11, 1979
WTO January 1, 1995

Djibouti

WTO May 31, 1995

Dominica

WTO January 1, 1995
Berne August 17, 1999

Dominican Republic

BAC October 31, 1912
UCC Geneva May 8, 1983
UCC Paris May 8, 1983
WTO March 9, 1995
Berne December 24, 1997 (Paris)

Ecuador

BAC August 31, 1914
UCC Geneva June 5, 1957
Phonogram Sept. 14, 1974
UCC Paris June 6, 1991
Berne October 9, 1991 (Paris)
WTO January 21, 1996

Egypt

Berne June 7, 1977 (Paris)
Phonogram April 23, 1978
WTO June 30, 1995

El Salvador

Bilateral June 30, 1908 (by
virtue of the Mexico City
Convention, 1902)
Phonogram February 9, 1979
UCC Geneva March 29, 1979
UCC Paris March 29, 1979
Berne February 19, 1994 (Paris)
WTO May 7, 1995

Equatorial Guinea

Berne June 26, 1997 (Paris)

Estonia

Berne October 26, 1994 (Paris)

Ethiopia

None

European Community

WTO January 1, 1995

Fiji

UCC Geneva October 10, 1970
Berne Dec. 1, 1971 (Brussels)
Phonogram April 18, 1973
WTO January 14, 1996

Finland

Berne April 1, 1928 (Paris)
Bilateral January 1, 1929
UCC Geneva April 16, 1963
Phonogram April 18, 1973
UCC Paris November 1, 1986
WTO January 1, 1995

France

Berne December 5, 1887 (Paris)
Bilateral July 1, 1891
UCC Geneva January 14, 1956
Phonogram April 18, 1973
UCC Paris July 10, 1974
WTO January 1, 1995

Gabon
Berne March 26, 1962 (Paris)
WTO January 1, 1995

Gambia, The
Berne March 7, 1993 (Paris)
WTO October 23, 1996

Georgia
UCC Geneva May 27, 1973*
Berne May 16, 1995 (Paris)
WTO October 6, 1999

Germany
Berne December 5, 1887 (Paris)
Bilateral April 16, 1892
UCC Geneva Sept. 16, 1955
Phonogram May 18, 1974
UCC Paris July 10, 1974
SAT August 25, 1979
WTO January 1, 1995

Ghana
UCC Geneva August 22, 1962
Berne October 11, 1991 (Paris)
WTO January 1, 1995

Greece
Berne Nov. 9, 1920 (Paris)
Bilateral March 1, 1932
UCC Geneva August 24, 1963
SAT October 22, 1991
Phonogram February 9, 1994
WTO January 1, 1995

Grenada
WTO February 22, 1996
Berne September 22, 1998 (Paris)

Guatemala
BAC March 28, 1913
UCC Geneva October 28, 1964
Phonogram February 1, 1977
WTO July 21, 1995
Berne July 28, 1997 (Paris)

Guinea
Berne Nov. 20, 1980 (Paris)
UCC Geneva Nov. 13, 1981
UCC Paris Nov. 13, 1981
WTO October 25, 1995

Guinea-Bissau
Berne July 22, 1991 (Paris)
WTO May 31, 1995

Guyana
Berne October 25, 1994 (Paris)
WTO January 1, 1995

Haiti
BAC November 27, 1919
UCC Geneva Sept. 16, 1955
Berne January 11, 1996 (Paris)
WTO January 30, 1996

Holy See (see Vatican City)

Honduras
BAC April 27, 1914
Berne January 25, 1990 (Paris)
Phonogram March 6, 1990
WTO January 1, 1995

Hong Kong
WTO January 1, 1995

Hungary
Bilateral October 16, 1912
Berne February 14, 1922 (Paris)
UCC Geneva January 23, 1971
(Paris)
UCC Paris July 10, 1974
Phonogram May 28, 1975
WTO January 1, 1995

Iceland
Berne Sept. 7, 1947 (Rome)
UCC Geneva Dec. 18, 1956
WTO January 1, 1995
Berne August 25, 1999 (Paris)

India
Berne April 1, 1928 (Paris)
Bilateral August 15, 1947
UCC Geneva January 21, 1958
Phonogram February 12, 1975
UCC Paris January 7, 1988
WTO January 1, 1995

Indonesia
Bilateral August 1, 1989
WTO January 1, 1995
Berne September 5, 1997 (Paris)

Iran
None

Iraq
None

Ireland
Berne Oct. 5, 1927 (Brussels)
Bilateral October 1, 1929
UCC Geneva January 20, 1959
WTO January 1, 1995

Israel
Bilateral May 15, 1948
Berne Mar. 24, 1950 (Brussels)
UCC Geneva Sept. 16, 1955
Phonogram May 1, 1978
WTO April 21, 1995

Italy
Berne December 5, 1887 (Paris)
Bilateral October 31, 1892
UCC Geneva January 24, 1957
Phonogram March 24, 1977
UCC Paris January 25, 1980
SAT July 7, 1981
WTO January 1, 1995

Ivory Coast (see Cote d'Ivoire)
Jamaica
Berne January 1, 1994 (Paris)
Phonogram January 11, 1994
WTO March 9, 1995

Japan
Berne July 15, 1899 (Paris)
UCC Geneva April 28, 1956
UCC Paris October 21, 1977
Phonogram October 14, 1978
WTO January 1, 1995

Jordan
Berne July 28, 1999 (Paris)

Kazakhstan
UCC Geneva May 27, 1973*
Berne April 12, 1999 (Paris)

Kenya
UCC Geneva Sept. 7, 1966
UCC Paris July 10, 1974
Phonogram April 21, 1976
SAT August 25, 1979
Berne June 11, 1993 (Paris)
WTO January 1, 1995

Kiribati
Unclear

Korea, Democratic People's Republic of
Unclear

Korea, Republic of
UCC Geneva October 1, 1987
UCC Paris October 1, 1987
Phonogram October 10, 1987
WTO January 1, 1995
Berne August 21, 1996 (Paris)

Kuwait
WTO January 1, 1995

Kyrgyz Republic
UCC Geneva May 27, 1973*
WTO December 20, 1998
Berne July 8, 1999 (Paris)

Laos
UCC Geneva Sept. 16, 1955

Latvia
Berne August 11, 1995 (Paris)
Phonogram August 23, 1997
WTO February 10, 1999

Lebanon
Berne Sept. 30, 1947 (Rome)
UCC Geneva Oct. 17, 1959

Lesotho
Berne Sept. 28, 1989 (Paris)
WTO May 31, 1995

Liberia
UCC Geneva July 27, 1956
Berne March 8, 1989 (Paris)

Libya
Berne Sept. 28, 1976 (Paris)

Liechtenstein
Berne July 30, 1931 (Brussels)
UCC Geneva January 22, 1959
WTO September 1, 1995
Berne September 23, 1999

Lithuania
Berne Dec. 14, 1994 (Paris)

Luxembourg
Berne June 20, 1888 (Paris)
Bilateral June 29, 1910
UCC Geneva October 15, 1955
Phonogram March 8, 1976
WTO January 1, 1995

Macau
WTO January 1, 1995

Macedonia (former Yugoslav Republic)
Berne Sept. 8, 1991 (Paris)
SAT November 17, 1991
UCC Geneva July 30, 1997
UCC Paris July 30, 1997
Phonogram March 2, 1998

Madagascar (Malagasy Republic)
Berne Jan. 1, 1966 (Brussels)
WTO November 17, 1995

Malawi
UCC Geneva October 26, 1985
Berne October 12, 1991 (Paris)
WTO May 31, 1995

Malaysia
Berne October 1, 1990 (Paris)
WTO January 1, 1995

Maldives
WTO May 31, 1995

Mali
Berne March 19, 1962 (Paris)
WTO May 31, 1995

Malta
Berne Sept. 21, 1964 (Rome)
UCC Geneva Nov. 19, 1968
WTO January 1, 1995

Mauritania
Berne February 6, 1973 (Paris)
WTO May 31, 1995

Mauritius
UCC Geneva May 12, 1968
Berne May 10, 1989 (Paris)
WTO January 1, 1995

Mexico
Bilateral February 27, 1896
UCC Geneva May 12, 1957
BAC April 24, 1964
Berne June 11, 1967 (Paris)
Phonogram Dec. 21, 1973
UCC Paris October 31, 1975
SAT August 25, 1979
WTO January 1, 1995

Moldova
UCC Geneva May 27, 1973*
Berne November 2, 1995 (Paris)
UCC Geneva July 18, 1997

Monaco
Berne May 30, 1889 (Paris)
Bilateral October 15, 1952
UCC Geneva Sept. 16, 1955
Phonogram Dec. 2, 1974
UCC Paris Dec. 13, 1974

Mongolia
WTO January 29, 1997
Berne March 12, 1998 (Paris)

Morocco
Berne June 16, 1917 (Paris)
UCC Geneva May 8, 1972
UCC Paris January 28, 1976
SAT June 30, 1983
WTO January 1, 1995

Mozambique
WTO August 26, 1995

Myanmar (formerly Burma)
WTO January 1, 1995

Namibia
Berne March 21, 1990 (Paris)
WTO January 1, 1995

Nauru
Unclear

Nepal
None

Netherlands
Bilateral Nov. 20, 1899
Berne Nov. 1, 1912 (Paris)
UCC Geneva June 22, 1967
UCC Paris Nov. 30, 1985
Phonogram Oct. 12, 1993
WTO January 1, 1995

New Zealand
Bilateral December 1, 1916
Berne April 24, 1928 (Rome)
UCC Geneva Sept. 11, 1964
Phonogram August 13, 1976
WTO January 1, 1995

Nicaragua
BAC December 15, 1913
UCC Geneva August 16, 1961
SAT August 25, 1979
WTO September 3, 1995

Niger
Berne May 2, 1962 (Paris)
UCC Geneva May 15, 1989
UCC Paris May 15, 1989
WTO December 13, 1996

Nigeria
UCC Geneva Feb. 14, 1962
Berne Sept. 14, 1993 (Paris)
WTO January 1, 1995

Norway
Berne Apr. 13, 1896 (Brussels)
Bilateral July 1, 1905
UCC Geneva January 23, 1963
UCC Paris August 7, 1974
Phonogram August 1, 1978
WTO January 1, 1995

Oman
Berne July 14, 1999 (Paris)

Pakistan
Berne July 5, 1948 (Rome)
UCC Geneva Sept. 16, 1955
WTO January 1, 1995

Palau
Unclear

Panama
BAC November 25, 1913
UCC Geneva October 17, 1962
Phonogram June 29, 1974
UCC Paris September 3, 1980
SAT September 25, 1985
Berne June 8, 1996 (Paris)

Papua New Guinea
WTO June 9, 1996

Paraguay
BAC September 20, 1917
UCC Geneva March 11, 1962
Phonogram February 13, 1979
Berne January 2, 1992 (Paris)
WTO January 1, 1995

Peru
BAC April 30, 1920
UCC Geneva October 16, 1963
UCC Paris July 22, 1985
SAT August 7, 1985
Phonogram August 24, 1985
Berne August 20, 1988 (Paris)
WTO January 1, 1995

Philippines
Bilateral October 21, 1948
Berne Aug. 1, 1951 (Brussels)
UCC status undetermined by
UNESCO (U.S. Copyright Office considers that UCC relations do not exist)
WTO January 1, 1995

Poland
Berne January 28, 1920 (Paris)
Bilateral February 16, 1927
UCC Geneva March 9, 1977
UCC Paris July 30, 1981
WTO July 1, 1995

Portugal
Bilateral July 20, 1893
Berne March 29, 1911 (Paris)
UCC Geneva Dec. 25, 1956
UCC Paris July 30, 1981
WTO January 1, 1995
SAT March 11, 1996

Qatar
WTO January 1, 1995

Romania
Berne January 1, 1927 (Rome)
Bilateral May 14, 1928
WTO January 1, 1995
Phonogram October 1, 1998

Russian Federation
UCC Geneva May 27, 1973
SAT December 25, 1991
UCC Paris March 9, 1995
Berne March 13, 1995 (Paris)
Phonogram March 13, 1995

Rwanda
Berne March 1, 1984 (Paris)
UCC Geneva Nov. 10, 1989
UCC Paris Nov. 10, 1989
WTO May 22, 1996

St. Christopher and Nevis
Berne April 9, 1995 (Paris)
WTO February 21, 1996

Saint Lucia
Berne August 24, 1993 (Paris)
WTO January 1, 1995

St. Vincent and the Grenadines
UCC Geneva April 22, 1985
UCC Paris April 22, 1985
WTO January 1, 1995
Berne August 29, 1995 (Paris)

San Marino
None

Sao Tomé and Principe
Unclear

Saudi Arabia
UCC Geneva July 13, 1994
UCC Paris July 13, 1994

Senegal
Berne August 25, 1962 (Paris)
UCC Geneva July 9, 1974
UCC Paris July 10, 1974
WTO January 1, 1995

Seychelles
Unclear

Sierra Leone
WTO July 23, 1995

Singapore
Bilateral May 18, 1987
WTO January 1, 1995
Berne December 21, 1998 (Paris)

Slovakia
UCC Geneva January 6, 1960
UCC Paris April 17, 1980
Berne January 1, 1993
Phonogram January 1, 1993
WTO January 1, 1995

Slovenia
UCC Geneva May 11, 1966
UCC Paris July 10, 1974
Berne June 25, 1991 (Paris)
SAT June 25, 1991
WTO July 30, 1995
Phonogram October 15, 1996

Solomon Islands
WTO July 26,1996

Somalia
Unclear

South Africa
Bilateral July 1, 1924
Berne Oct. 3, 1928 (Brussels)
WTO January 1, 1995

Soviet Union (see **Russian Federation**)

Spain
Berne Dec. 5, 1887 (Paris)
Bilateral July 10, 1895
UCC Geneva Sept. 16, 1955
UCC Paris July 10, 1974
Phonogram August 24, 1974
WTO January 1, 1995

Sri Lanka (formerly **Ceylon**)
Berne July 20, 1959 (Rome)
UCC Geneva January 25, 1984
UCC Paris January 25, 1984
WTO January 1, 1995

Sudan
Unclear

Suriname
Berne Feb. 23, 1977 (Paris)
WTO January 1, 1995

Swaziland
WTO January 1, 1995
Berne December 14, 1998 (Paris)

Sweden
Berne August 1, 1904 (Paris)
Bilateral June 1, 1911
UCC Geneva July 1, 1961
Phonogram April 18, 1973
UCC Paris July 10, 1974
WTO January 1, 1995

Switzerland
Berne Dec. 5, 1887 (Paris)
Bilateral July 1, 1891
UCC Geneva March 30, 1956
UCC Paris Sept. 21, 1993
SAT September 24, 1993
Phonogram Sept. 30, 1993
WTO July 1, 1995

Syria
Unclear

Tajikistan
UCC Geneva May 27, 1973*
Berne March 9, 2000 (Paris)

Tanzania
Berne July 25, 1994 (Paris)
WTO January 1, 1995

Thailand
Bilateral September 1, 1921
Berne July 17, 1931 (Berlin)
WTO January 1, 1995

Togo
Berne April 30, 1975 (Paris)
WTO May 31, 1995

Tonga
None

Trinidad and Tobago
Berne August 16, 1988 (Paris)
UCC Geneva August 19, 1988
UCC Paris August 19, 1988
Phonogram October 1, 1988
WTO March 1, 1995
SAT November 1, 1996

Tunisia
Berne December 5, 1887 (Paris)
UCC Geneva June 19, 1969
UCC Paris June 10, 1975
WTO March 29, 1995

Turkey
Berne Jan. 1, 1952 (Brussels)
WTO March 26, 1995

Turkmenistan
UCC Geneva May 27, 1973*

Tuvalu
Unclear

Uganda
WTO January 1, 1995

Ukraine
UCC Geneva May 27, 1973
Berne October 25, 1995 (Paris)

United Arab Emirates
WTO April 10, 1996

United Kingdom
Berne Dec. 5, 1887 (Paris)
Bilateral July 1, 1891
UCC Geneva Sept. 27, 1957
Phonogram April 18, 1973
UCC Paris July 10, 1974
WTO January 1, 1995

Upper Volta (see Burkina Faso)

Uruguay
BAC December 17, 1919
Berne July 10, 1967 (Paris)
Phonogram January 18, 1983
UCC Geneva April 12, 1993
UCC Paris April 12, 1993
WTO January 1, 1995

Uzbekistan
UCC Geneva May 27, 1973*

Vanuatu
Unclear

Vatican City (Holy See)
Berne Sept. 12, 1935 (Paris)
UCC Geneva Oct. 5, 1955
Phonogram July 18, 1977
UCC Paris May 6, 1980

Venezuela
UCC Geneva Sept. 12, 1935 (Paris)
Phonogram Nov. 18, 1982
Berne Dec. 30, 1982 (Paris)
WTO January 1, 1995
UCC Paris February 11, 1997

Vietnam
Bilateral December 23, 1998

Western Samoa
Unclear

Yemen (Aden)
Unclear

Yemen (San'a)
None

Yugoslavia
Berne June 17, 1930 (Paris)
UCC Geneva May 11, 1966
UCC Paris July 10, 1974
SAT August 25, 1979

Zaire (see Democratic Republic of Congo)

Zambia
UCC Geneva June 1, 1965
Berne January 2, 1992 (Paris)
WTO January 1, 1995

Zimbabwe
Berne April 18, 1980 (Rome)
WTO March 3, 1995

* All countries that were formerly part of the Soviet Union agreed in bilateral agreements with the U.S. that they were successor states to the U.S.S.R.'s membership in the UCC effective from May 27, 1973.

In 1994, President Clinton signed the Uruguay Round Agreements Act (URAA) which added a new provision to the Copyright Law to restore copyright in certain foreign works. The U.S. Copyright Office then issued final regulations establishing procedures that govern the filing of Notices of Intent to Enforce copyright (NIEs) and the registering of copyright claims to restored works as required by the URAA. The Act automatically restores copyright for certain foreign works effective January 1, 1996. Although restoration is automatic, the copyright owner may file a Notice of Intent to Enforce the Restored Copyright with the Copyright Office in order to enforce rights against so-called reliance parties (those who acquired copies of the restored work before restoration and wish to continue exploiting it). A country that is eligible for restoration of copyright is a nation, other than the United States, that is a member of the Berne Convention, or a member of the World Trade Organization, or is the subject of a presidential proclamation declaring its eligibility.

In order for a work to be restored, it must meet certain requirements:

1. It is not in the public domain in its source country through expiration of the term of protection.
2. It is in the public domain in the United States due to noncompliance with formalities imposed by U.S. Copyright law (i.e. no copyright notice, no renewal, etc.).
3. It has at least one author or rightholder who was, at the time the work was created, a national or domiciliary of an eligible country.
4. If published, it was first published in an eligible country and was not published in the U.S. during the 30-day period following publication in such eligible country.

For further information contact: U.S. Copyright Office, Office of the General Counsel; telephone: 202-707-8380; facsimile: 202-707-8366.

Chapter 7
SAMPLE LETTERS AND CONTRACTS

SAMPLE "NO RIGHTS" (NR) LETTER

Mr. John Smith
Textbook Assistant
University of Camelot
Camelot 00000

RE: Title, by Author

Dear Mr. Smith:

Thank you for your recent request to use material from the referenced title. Unfortunately, we do not control rights for the material you wish to use. This material was originally published elsewhere and we have permission to use it in our work only. Please check the acknowledgments section of your text for the proper copyright owner.

Sincerely,

SAMPLE PUBLIC DOMAIN (PD) LETTER

Mr. John Smith
Textbook Assistant
University of Camelot
Camelot 00000

Dear Mr. Smith:

Thank you for your request to reprint material from one of our texts. The material you have requested ["PAGE INFORMATION - TITLE, AUTHOR"] is in the public domain in the United States. Therefore, the granting of permission is unnecessary here.

Sincerely,

SAMPLE CONTRACT FOR PUBLICATION PERMISSION

Mr. John Smith
Textbook Assistant
University of Camelot
Camelot 00000

Dear Mr. Smith:

We are pleased to grant permission to you for the reprinting of:
[PAGE INFORMATION]
From: [YOUR TEXT]
For use in: [THEIR TEXT (PUT THEIR AUTHOR NAME HERE ALSO)].

This permission is a one-time, non-exclusive grant for English language use as described in this letter, in the following territory only: [World]

This permission is subject to the following conditions:

1. Payment on or before initial publication of your book of the following fee: $FEE
2. Each copy containing our material that you reproduce or distribute must bear the following copyright notice:
   "Copyright © [COPYRIGHT DATE]
   From [YOUR TEXT]
   By [YOUR AUTHOR(S)]
   Reprinted with permission of [PUBLISHER]."
3. Permission is granted for print usage only. No permission is granted for any other uses, including any electronic ones.
4. Our receipt of one copy of your book, upon publication.

If these terms are acceptable, please sign and date the enclosed copy of this letter and return it to my attention. This permission becomes effective upon our receipt of the signed contract.

When sending copy of the signed contract, payment and copy of your book, please make clear reference to our title and author, and to the date of our permissions agreement. Also, please address all envelopes and packages to: _____. Thank you for your attention in these matters.

Should you elect not to use this material, please inform us so that we may clear our records.

Sincerely,

AGREED:_____
DATE: _____

_____We have elected not to use this material.

SAMPLE "NEED ADDITIONAL INFORMATION" LETTER

Mr. John Smith
Textbook Assistant
University of Camelot
Camelot 00000

Dear Mr. Smith:

Thank you for your request to reproduce material from one of our texts. Before I can consider this request, however, I need the following information:

____ title of text
____ author/editor/translator of text
___ edition number and/or copyright year (or a copy of the copyright page, if this title is very dated)
_X_ page numbers as they appear in our book
____ number of copies to be made
____ name of professor requesting this material
____ name of the course this material is for
____ semester material is needed for
____ name of school
___ ISBN
____ author and title of work in which the material will appear
____ publisher and publication date of the work in which the material will appear

I look forward to hearing from you.

Sincerely,

SAMPLE "REFERRAL" LETTER

Mr. John Smith
Textbook Assistant
University of Camelot
Camelot 00000

RE: Title, by Author

Dear Mr. Smith:

Thank you for your recent request to use material from the referenced title. Unfortunately, we do not control the requested rights for this title. According to our records, rights are held by:

[REFERRAL ADDRESS]

Sincerely,

SAMPLE PERMISSION LICENSE:
COMMERCIAL ELECTRONIC USE

DATE: XXXXXX
TO: XXXXXXX ("Licensee")

Licensed Material:
Author:
Title:
Exact Material:
Fee:

Licensee Work:
Author:
Title:
Publisher:
Format: Internet web site/CD-ROM/print (CHOOSE ALL APPLICABLE)
Distribution: world/North American/U.S.; English/all languages

Licensor hereby grants XXXXX the non-exclusive right to use the Licensed Material as outlined and to reproduce and distribute the Licensor Material in the Licensee Work under the following conditions only:

1. No changes may be made to the Licensed Material without the prior written consent of Licensor.

2. Licensee will provide to Licensor the URL and password for any web site in which the Licensed Material appears.

3. Licensor makes no representations or warranties as to the accuracy of any information contained in the Licensed Material, including any warranties of merchantability or fitness for a particular purpose. In no event shall Licensor have any liability to any party for special, incidental, tort, or consequential damages arising out of or in connection with the Licensee Material, even if Licensor has been advised of the possibility of such damages. All persons provided with the Licensee Material must be provided with written notice of this disclaimer and limitation liability.

4. A credit and copyright notice for the Licensed Material shall be visible each time the end-user initiates access to any screen or page containing any of the Licensed Material. Such credit shall include the following copyright notice and statement: Reproduced by permission of XXXXX.

5. In consideration of this permission, Licensee shall pay Licensor a fee of XXXXX within sixty (60) days from the date of this Agreement. A check payable to XXXXX shall be sent to the address first set forth above.

6. This permission does not cover the use of any third-party copyrighted material, including but not limited to photographs and other illustrations, which appears in the Licensed Material with a credit to other sources. Written permission to use such material must be obtained from the cited source.

7. Licensor shall have the right to terminate this Agreement immediately upon written notice to Licensee if Licensee is in material breach of this Agreement.
8. Licensee shall indemnify Licensor from any damages, lawsuits, claims, liabilities, costs, charges, and expenses, including attorney's fees, relating to its use of the Licensor Material.
9. This Agreement incorporates the parties' entire agreement with respect to its subject matter. This Agreement may be amended only by a writing signed by both parties. Licensee may not assign this Agreement or any rights granted hereunder to any third party.

BY: _____

LICENSEE: _____

BY: _____

TITLE: _____

DATE: _____

SAMPLE "NO FEE" LETTER

Mr. John Smith
Textbook Assistant
University of Camelot
Camelot 00000

Dear Mr. Smith:

We are pleased to grant permission for the reprinting of the material you have requested as per attached, for this one-time usage. This permission does include world rights. No fee will be required, but please make acknowledgments to the author and work and to [PUBLISHER], as indicated in our book.

Thank you.

Sincerely,

SAMPLE PERMISSION LICENSE:
CLASSROOM ELECTRONIC USE

DATE: XXXXXXX
TO: XXXXXXX ("Licensee")

Licensed Material:
Author:
Title:
Exact Material:
Fee:

Purpose of Reproduction:
Course:
School:
Format: PASSWORD PROTECTED web site/closed campus LAN/closed campus electronic reserve system/CD-ROM/print (CHOOSE ONE OR MORE)
Number of Copies (if applicable):
Semester:
Distribution: course/professor/semester

Licensor hereby grants XXXXX the non-exclusive right to use the Licensed Material as outlined and to reproduce and distribute the Licensor Material as outlined under purpose of reproduction above, under the following conditions only:

1. No changes may be made to the Licensed Material without the prior written consent of Licensor.
2. Licensee will provide to Licensor the URL and password for any web site in which the Licensed Material appears.
3. Licensor makes no representations or warranties as to the accuracy of any information contained in the Licensed Material, including any warranties of merchantability or fitness for a particular purpose. In no event shall Licensor have any liability to any party for special, incidental, tort, or consequential damages arising out of or in connection with the Licensee Material, even if Licensor has been advised of the possibility of such damages. All persons provided with the Licensee Material must be provided with written notice of this disclaimer and limitation liability.
4. A credit and copyright notice for the Licensed Material shall be visible each time the end-user initiates access to any screen or page containing any of the Licensed Material. Such credit shall include the following copyright notice and statement: Reproduced by permission of XXXXX.
5. In consideration of this permission, Licensee shall pay Licensor a fee of XXXXX within sixty (60) days from the date of this Agreement. A check payable to XXXXX shall be sent to the address first set forth above.
6. This permission does not cover the use of any third-party copyrighted material, including but not limited to photographs and other illustrations, which appears in the Licensed Material with a credit to other sources. Written permission to use such material must be obtained from the cited source.

7. Licensor shall have the right to terminate this Agreement immediately upon written notice to Licensee if Licensee is in material breach of this Agreement.
8. Licensee shall indemnify Licensor from any damages, lawsuits, claims, liabilities, costs, charges, and expenses, including attorney's fees, relating to its use of the Licensor Material.
9. This Agreement incorporates the parties' entire agreement with respect to its subject matter. This Agreement may be amended only by a writing signed by both parties. Licensee may not assign this Agreement or any rights granted hereunder to any third party.

BY: _____
LICENSEE: _____

BY: _____
TITLE: _____
DATE: _____

SAMPLE PERCENT LETTER

Mr. John Smith
Textbook Assistant
University of Camelot
Camelot 00000

Dear Mr. Smith:

I am sorry to inform you that we cannot grant permission to reproduce the pages that you have requested. These pages comprise a large portion of our book. As such, permission cannot be granted. We suggest the book should be purchased instead.

Sincerely,

SAMPLE CONTRACT FOR CLASSROOM PERMISSION

TO:

When signed by you, this document will constitute a contract by which we are granting you non-transferrable, non-exclusive permission to make and distribute photocopies of:

from: (title/author)
for classroom use: (instructor/course name/school name/semester term)

This permission is subject to the following conditions:

1. You must promptly sign and return this permission.
2. You must pay us a fee of $_____ per copy, with a minimum fee of $__ by [date]. If you do not make this payment by the deadline, this permission will become void.
3. Each copy of our material that you make or distribute must bear the following copyright notice and acknowledgment:
    Copyright © ____ by
    From _____
    By _____
    Reproduced by Permission of [PUBLISHER]
4. This permission extends only to reproduction of copies for distribution to students in the course specified above during the semester or school term specified above. Any other use (including, but not limited to, use for other courses, semesters or terms) requires additional permission from us.
5. No more than _____ copies may be reproduced or distributed without additional permission from us.
6. This permission extends only to material owned or controlled by us. Please check the credits in our book for material in which the copyright is not owned by us or our author. You should apply to the owner(s) of the copyright in such material that is not ours for permission to reproduce or otherwise use it.

The terms of the above permission are accepted and agreed to.

By: _____
(Signature)

_____
(Print name and title of person signing)

_____
(Date)

___We have elected NOT to use the material requested:

Appendix A
FOR FURTHER INFORMATION

BOOKS

Association of American Publishers, *Focus on Rights*, New York, NY, 1995.

Association of American Publishers, *The Handbook of International Rights*, New York, NY, 1991.

Brinson, Dianne J. and Radcliffe, Mark F., *Multimedia Law Handbook*. Menlo Park, CA, Ladera Press, 1994.

Carter, Mary E., *Electronic Highway Robbery: An Artist's Guide to Copyrights in the Digital Era*, Berkeley, CA, Peachpit Press, 1996.

Crawford, Tad and Lyons, Tony, *The Writer's Legal Guide*, New York, NY, Allworth Press, 1996.

Jassin, Lloyd and Schechter, Steven, *The Copyright Permission and Libel Handbook: A Step by Step Guide for Writers, Editors and Publishers*, New York, NY, John Wiley and Sons, 1998.

LMP (Literary Market Place), New Providence, NJ, R.R. Bowker. Published annually.

Norwick, Kenneth P. and Chasen, Jerry Simon, *The Rights of Authors, Artists, and Other Creative People*, Carbondale, IL, Southern Illinois University Press, 1992.

Owen, Lynette, *Selling Rights*, 3rd Edition, London, Routledge, October 1997 (2nd Edition, 1994).

Perle, E. Gabriel and Williams, John Taylor, *The Publishing Law Handbook*, Englewood Cliffs, NJ, Prentice Hall Law & Business, 1995.

Smedinghoff, Thomas J. (ed.), *Online Law: The SPA's Legal Guide to Doing Business on the Internet*, Reading, MA, Addison-Wesley Developers Press, 1996.

Stim, Richard, *Getting Permission: How to License & Clear Copyrighted Materials Online and Off,* Berkley, CA, Nolo Press, 2000.

Strong, William S., *The Copyright Book: Practical Guide,* 4th ed., Cambridge, MA, MIT Press, 1993.

University of Chicago Press, *The Chicago Manual of Style,* Chicago, IL, University of Chicago Press, 1993.

ON-LINE

The following are some sites that offer good copyright information, plus links to many other intellectual property resources. [Note that the following addresses were current as of May 2000.]

AAP
http://www.publishers.org

ASCAP [search database]
http://www.ascap.com

BMI [search database]
http://www.bmi.com

COPYRIGHT CLEARANCE CENTER
http://www.copyright.com

COPYRIGHT MANAGEMENT CENTER - INDIANA UNIVERSITY
http://www.iupui.edu/~copyinfo

COPYRIGHT OFFICE [Circulars, Searches post 1972]
http://www.loc.gov/copyright

COPYRIGHT WEBSITE
http://www.benedict.com

CORNELL LAW SCHOOL, THE LEGAL INFORMATION INSTITUTE
http://www.law.cornell.edu

FAIR USE AND COPYRIGHT
http://fairuse.stanford.edu

GENERAL INFORMATION ABOUT COPYRIGHTS
http://www.patents.com/copyrigh.sht

INTELLECTUAL PROPERTY MALL PAGE [Franklin Pierce Law Center]
http://www.fplc.edu/IPMALL

INTERNATIONAL INTELLECTUAL PROPERTY ALLIANCE (IIPA)
http://www.iipa.com

INTERNATIONAL PUBLISHERS ASSOCIATION (IPA)
http://www.ipa-uie.org

KUESTERLAW THE TECHNOLOGY LAW RESOURCE
http://www.kuesterlaw.com

LIBRARY OF CONGRESS
http://www.loc.gov

NATIONAL ASSOCIATION OF COLLEGE STORES (NACS)
http://www.nacs.org

UNIVERSITY LIBRARIES AND SCHOLARLY COMMUNICATION
http://www.lib.virginia.edu/

US ISSN CENTER HOME PAGE (LIBRARY OF CONGRESS)
http://www.loc.gov/issn

WWW VIRTUAL LIBRARY - LAW
http://www.law.indiana.edu

Appendix B
DEFINITIONS

Ancillaries: material that accompanies or relates to a main text, such as student guides, instructor's manuals, educational software, transparency masters, etc.

Anthology: a collection of selected works produced as one unit. Copyright may be claimed in the unit, even if copyright to the individual pieces are held by others. *Course packs* are a form of an anthology.

Berne Convention: The Berne Convention for the Protection of Literary and Artistic Works, a multilateral copyright treaty administered by the World Intellectual Property Organization (WIPO). The Convention, with about 120 members, offers copyright protection based on "national treatment," a principle requiring works of foreign creators of member countries to receive at a minimum, the same level of protection accorded to local authors.

Best edition: the edition that the Library of Congress determines to be the most suitable for copyright deposit, usually meaning the highest quality edition.

CD-ROM: Compact Disc with Read Only Memory, which can be used in a computer system.

Common law: Law established by the courts and precedent rather than by statutes enacted federally or through state legislatures.

Compilation: A work created by the collection and assembling of preexisting materials, often including facts and data, coordinated or arranged in such a way that the resulting work as a whole constitutes an original work of authorship. Collective works are included in this term.

Copy: One of multiple physical manifestations of a work. A copy can include manuscripts, pages of magazines, books, posters, canvases, computer files, and images stored on any digital media (DVD, CD-ROM, flash memory, or a computer hard drive).

Course packs: *compilations* or *anthologies* of photocopied selections from various sources that are bound or left unbound and distributed to students.

Credit: a line of text, usually at the bottom of the page or screen or on a separate acknowledgments page or screen, identifying the copyright date and owner, and stating that the material was used by permission.

Custom publishing: a method of providing individualized content. Consumers can select and combine material, usually residing in electronic form in a database, to meet their specific needs. The selections are normally printed and bound.

Derivative Work: A work that is based on the additional authorship added to one or more preexisting works where such original works have been transformed into a new work, such as translations, abridgments, adaptations for film or theater, photographs or artwork that has been electronically manipulated, etc.

Fair use: A limitation on the exclusive rights of the copyright owner that allows copies of a work to be made without permission. Although there are no specifics on what fair use is, and determinations must be made on a case-by-case basis, the copyright law lists four factors to consider in making the determination: the purpose and character of the use; the nature of the copyrighted work; the amount and substantiality of what is used relative to the whole; and the effect of the use on the potential market for the copyrighted work.

Infringement: A violation of any of the exclusive rights of the copyright owner. A copyright infringement may be committed when someone uses a work that is not in the public domain in one of the many ways reserved to the copyright owner without that owner's permission.

Internet: A worldwide, decentralized series of interconnected networks using a common communications technology.

Joint work: A work prepared by two or more authors with the intention that their contributions be merged into inseparable or interdependent parts of a unitary whole.

License: A legal agreement granting permission to exercise specified rights to a work.

Publication: A work is published when it is distributed or offered to the public by sale, rental, performance, display, or other methods making one or multiple copies available.

Public domain: A work whose copyright has expired or is not otherwise eligible for copyright protection, such as works by the U.S. government. These works may be copied without restriction in that particular country.

Registration: The making of a registration of a claim to copyright in a work with the Copyright Office by filling out the appropriate form, paying a fee, and providing a copy (or copies) of the work. Registration, although not necessary for copyright protection, provides certain legal, statutory, and commercial benefits.

Royalty: A portion of income from copies sold for a licensed edition. Royalties benefit the author/creator as well as the rights holder.

Scanning: A technology that converts printed text into digital form, where the text is ultimately converted into a manipulatable file of characters. It can also be done by merely depicting the page image in electronic form.

Subsidiary rights: Rights beyond the initial grant of rights to publish a work in a specific territory. These include paperback, book club, serial, anthology, volume, commercial, and other such rights.

Work made for hire: A copyrightable work that is prepared by an employee within the scope of employment, or a work that is specially ordered or commissioned and fits into one of nine enumerated categories. The employer or commissioner of the work is considered the author for copyright purposes in the United States.